RURAL DEVELOPMENT AND EDUCATION

RURAL DEVELOPMENT AND EDUCATION

(In 2 Volumes)

Challenges of Rural Education

(Volume-1)

Editor

Dr. M.L. Dhawan

ISHA BOOKS

DELHI-110 033

Rural Development and Education

ISBN: 81-8205-055-3 (Set)
ISBN: 81-8205-056-1 (Vol. 1)

Published in 2004 in India by
Isha Books, D-43, Prithviraj Road,
Adarsh Nagar, Delhi-110 033

Laser Typesetting at : Shree Vaishnavi Creations, Delhi
Printed at : Chawla Offset Press, Delhi

Contents

Preface

Over the last decade, efforts have been under way to help rural education be more responsive to the growth and survival needs of the rural communities. These efforts have been driven by numerous factors and trends effecting rural communities, often in deleterious ways. For example, low population density and geographic isolation have made rural communities especially vulnerable to the economic, social, and environmental trends emerging from the world's move away from local manufacturing and resource based industries, toward a multi-national, global economy.

Despite these downturns, rural people remain a vital to all nations. Rural communities often reflect such valued norms as helping one's neighbour, strong work ethics, low crime rates, environmental quality etc. Educational institutions represent an important element in the rural community's social capital. Too often, however, local schools have seen themselves only as an educational resource for the community's youth. Ironically, the community has generally been viewed solely as a revenue resource for sustaining operation of the schools.

Many rural advocates feel a promising direction for revitalization and survival rests with the social capital that can be created by building and sustaining strong linkages between the community and the school. Rural communities may have a head start in developing these linkages because schools have traditionally played a central role in the life of the communities. Besides providing for basic education, they have often served as a cultural and training centres and as centres for development planning in rural areas.

Various facets of rural education are analytically discussed in the present book. Students, teachers, educationists and educational administrators besides policy planners and teacher-trainers will find it as most useful and informative.

Editor

1

Rural Education and Community Development

Over the last decade, efforts have been under way to help rural schools be more responsive to the growth and survival needs of their communities. These efforts have been driven by numerous factors and trends effecting rural communities, often in deleterious ways.

For example, low population density and geographic isolation have made rural communities especially vulnerable to the economic, social, and environmental trends emerging from the nation's move away from local manufacturing and resource based industries, toward a multi-national, global economy. Mining, logging, agriculture, and manufacturing, once robust industries in rural America, have come to a near standstill, leaving high rates of unemployment with attendant problems of social and economic distress. Despite these downturns, rural America and its people remain a vital national asset.

Rural communities often reflect such valued norms as

helping one's neighbor, strong work ethics, low crime rates, environmental quality, and a we can do it community spirit that provides fertile ground for creating a capacity for revitalization. Of paramount importance has been the role of school resources in assisting community development efforts, especially its youth.

Although the school has generally played an active role in rural communities, it has often been constrained by educator and community conceptions of schooling that limit learning opportunities within the perimeters of the school's walls and the textbooks. Community development reflects any effort designed to improve the economic, social or environmental well-being of the community. However, community development specialists have tended to focus on economics and thus failing to recognize the interdependent nature of these three dimensions.

In the past, it may have been the case that focusing on economic issues was all that was needed to keep rural communities viable. But with the globalization of the economy and the rapid urbanization of rural areas, there has been an accompanying break down in community solidarity. Businesses have closed, the young and well educated are leaving for metropolitan areas, and many social services, including schools, have been regionalized or consolidated as cost cutting measures.

These trends have lead to high levels of unemployment and the deterioration of rural economic, social, and environmental well-being. Recent evidence seems to suggest that if community development efforts are to have a chance of success, they need to address the importance of social capital, especially for the long-term maintenance of successful change efforts.

Clearly, the school represents an important element in the community's social capital. Too often, however, local schools have seen themselves only as an educational resource for the community's youth. Ironically, the community has generally been viewed solely as a revenue resource for sustaining operation of the schools.

Many rural advocates feel a promising direction for revitalization and survival rests with the social capital that can be created by building and sustaining strong linkages between the community and the school. Rural communities may have a head start in developing these linkages because schools have traditionally played a central role in the life of the communities.

Besides providing for basic education, they have often served as a cultural center in the community where athletics, drama programs, music, and other social activities play a vital part in community life and identity. However, building a strong partnership with the school for community development purposes remains a major challenge because it is not generally viewed as a traditional element of schooling.

Some schools and communities have met this challenge and managed to restructure elements of schooling to provide experiences for students that serve both educational needs and community development goals. In the north central cascades of Washington State, the Methow School District implemented a comprehensive community-based learning project called, Community as a Classroom.

A local resident coordinates more than 200 activities and classes taught by community volunteers to high school students. Students benefit from their involvement in multiple ways. They learn valuable workplace competencies, opportunities to test out their vocational and recreational interests, and to develop meaningful relationships with the adults in their community.

Most students also discover summer and part-time employment opportunities through the positive relationships they establish with local businesses and organizations. Moreover, the community benefits in multiple ways as well. Local businesses are able to tap into a reliable employment pool. Students provide meaningful opportunities for adults to teach and return something to the community. Students also provide community service and development help to local groups and organizations needing assistance in completing projects.

Rural communities illustrate how strong linkages can be built between the school and the community which serve to strengthen and sustain a mutually viable future. Teacher, administrative, and school board action provided a framework of permission within which community-based learning opportunities could happen. Neither students, teachers, administrators, nor community members acted in isolation. Changes in their respective communities occurred because they worked together and because adults recognized the value of youth for the future of their communities.

Three unique, yet overlapping approaches that build strong linkages between schools and communities have been identified. Each approach reflects learning opportunities and experiences that cross boundaries which have traditionally separated the community as a place of learning from the school. The first approach reflects the school as a community center, serving as both a resource for lifelong learning and as a vehicle for the delivery of a wide range of services.

School resources such as facilities, technology, and a well-educated staff can provide a range of educational and retraining opportunities for the community. An early manifestation of this approach was the community school movement of the 70s where educational opportunities ranging from day care to adult literacy were offered. In recent years, the idea of school as community center has resurfaced in the concept of integrated family services, where the school serves as a linking agent for the social service needs of rural youth and families.

These may include health screening, day care, and dental treatment. In Saco, Montana, the school district has been funded for a fiber optic network linking three remote communities together. The network will provide training for health professionals and fire departments. Moreover, it will network schools and communities together thus facilitating the sharing of resources.

A second approach uses the community as curriculum, emphasizing the study of community in all its various dimensions. Students generate information for community development by conducting needs assessments, studying and monitoring environmental and land-use patterns, and by documenting local history through interviews and photo essays.

The most comprehensive approach to community as curriculum in terms of sustained use nationally is the Foxfire network which provides teacher development and a teacher support network. Foxfire engages students in learning about their community through direct encounters with its history.

A third approach, school-based enterprise (SBE), places a major emphasis on developing entrepreneurial skills whereby students not only identify potential service needs in their rural communities, but actually establish a business to address those needs. Sher and DeLargy have turned the SBE concept into a comprehensive curriculum program for rural schools called REAL (Rural Entrepreneurship through Action Learning).

With the help of REAL, students have set up shoe repair, a delicatessen, and day-care businesses, providing both employment and filling a service not formally available. These three interrelated approaches provide a way to think about how schools and communities can work together for their mutual benefit.

The value of these community-based learning experiences

are the long-term benefits of leadership development, a renewed sense of civic responsibility, and a revitalized sense of community. However, because these approaches reflect a departure from the more traditional ways educators and communities have viewed curriculum, it becomes imperative to develop policy support from those organizations and individuals whose endorsement may be critical to the success of program efforts.

Many elements of the community and school need attention if efforts to link them together for development purposes are to be implemented and sustained over time. Most important, developing a support base in the community provides a strong foundation upon which to build lasting community-based learning experiences. Secondly, engaging teachers in curriculum work that links student service activities in the classroom with projects in the community appears to be critically important.

Finally, long-term sustainability of a community-school development partnership should be a primary aim. For the test of success will be whether a new and empowering partnership between the community and school has been created that can meaningfully impact the lives of rural youth and adults over an extended period of time.

Moreover, it needs to be kept in mind that the changes implied in building a community-school development partnership where students engage in community-based learning experiences are essentially questions about changing the way schools go about preparing rural youth for the future.

By starting with the premise that community needs and school needs are interrelated, we create opportunities to explore ways that students and the school could address community needs while helping students learn valuable life skills. This is as true or even more true for rural areas as it is for urban areas.

Rural and Remote Education

Rural and remote areas of Queensland make a major contribution to the Queensland economy. The continuing strength of our rural economy depends on a vibrant, skilled workforce capable of sustaining rural development while at the same time embracing global trends.

Quality education services in the bush are an important part of this future. Over half of all state schools in Queensland are located in rural and remote areas. These schools cater for approximately one-third of all students enrolled in the state school system. Living and learning in rural and remote areas offers unique advantages and opportunities for students and teachers.

In many country areas, the local school is the hub of the community and the site for many community activities. As enrolments and populations are often small, school communities tend to be tight-knit and supportive. Teachers are likely to know students and their extended families well, and students are likely to know their peers well, both in a school and a community context. School environments in rural and remote areas are often characterised by:

— *Well-developed pastoral relationships with the local community;*

— *A strong sense of belonging to the school and the broader community;*

— *A sense of safety; and*

— *Creative partnerships with local community organisations, businesses and industries for building innovative learning environments and experiences for students. Partnerships being fostered out of a commitment to the wellbeing of fellow community members.*

Queensland has always been regarded as a world leader in the provision of quality education services to students living in rural and remote areas. Schools in these areas of our state are among the most innovative in Queensland and, in many cases, Australia. To maintain its leadership in the field of rural and remote education, Education Queensland has a continuing commitment to identify new challenges as they arise and to develop innovative and responsive education and training solutions.

Schools will work actively with their local communities to identify issues of mutual concern and generate innovative responses that build on community capacity. Education Queensland will foster relationships and partnerships with local community groups, government and non-government agencies and industry to support schools in delivering flexible individualised learning and training opportunities for young people in rural, remote and Indigenous communities.

The Rural and Remote Education Framework for Action recognises that the characteristics of rural and remote communities are diverse, and that the learning contexts and needs of students in these communities are varied. Rural and remote education in Queensland encompasses a number of settings including:

— *Distance education;*

— *Small primary schools;*

— *Schools in provincial towns;*

As well as the more traditional schooling subjects, learning programs will include Vocational Education and Training conducted in schools and in workplaces; specialised programs for students with disabilities; programs for students with a language other than English as their first language and support for students who undertake their learning away from home.

Education Queensland continues to support and enhance distance education programs and delivery methods for students who live in locations where attending a school is impossible, and as a way to increase the range of curriculum options of students in small secondary schools.

There are over 500 small primary schools in rural and remote areas of Queensland, demonstrating Education Queensland's commitment to education service delivery in small communities across the state. While these schools face unique challenges in attracting and retaining staff, in managing multi-age curriculum delivery and meeting administrative requirements, they offer highly individualised learning contexts for students in small communities.

Successful models for collaboration in curriculum planning, resource management and effective use of local expertise have been implemented in many provincial centres. Further opportunities exist for innovative partnerships and alliances across state and non-state schools and across primary and secondary schools.

The Rural and Remote Education Framework for Action builds on the principles and intent of the National Framework for Rural and Remote Education developed by the MCEETYA Taskforce on Rural and Remote Education and adapts its essential enablers to address the key challenges for education in rural and remote areas of Queensland. Targets and actions are being developed in the following priority action areas:

— *Relevant and Engaged Learning;*

— *Respecting Cultural Diversity;*

— *ICTs and Multimodal Delivery;*

— *Personnel and Workforce Capability; and*

— *Environments and Resourcing.*

To maintain and improve the attendance, retention and achievement of students in rural and remote communities, the curriculum must be relevant and engaging and meet the diverse needs of students. MCEETYA research shows that curriculum best meets the needs of rural and remote students when:

— *Programs are developed in partnership with the local community that are responsive to local community needs and meet the requirements of a global society;*

— *Curriculum is aligned with the requirements of the National Goals of Schooling and are appropriately applied to the local context; and*

— *Educational options and pathways in schools are designed to articulate with training and employment pathways.*

The Framework for Action addresses specifically the need to:

— *Improve attendance rates for rural and remote students;*

— *Improve learning and training pathways and retention rates, especially in the senior phase of learning;*

— *'Unclutter ' the curriculum to provide more space and time for students to achieve deeper understanding and higher levels of engagement in learning;*

— *Promote greater curriculum consistency across classrooms and schools, and greater continuity across year levels; and*

— *Provide more engaging and intellectually challenging learning and teaching.*

To deliver improved levels of achievement and respect for cultural diversity for all students in rural and remote schools. Diversity is at the core of every school community. Education Queensland is committed to recognising and valuing diversity in our schools and workplaces and promoting inclusiveness in our everyday practices so that all Queenslanders can participate and succeed in education, training and employment.

To increase and extend the education and training options of students in rural and remote areas using ICTs and a range of curriculum delivery methods. Distance and population size and range of choice mean that not all curricula will be available through face-to-face methods. The diversity of rural and remote locations needing quality education services requires a multimodal approach to delivery.

While ICTs are strategic modes for extending students ' access to education and training options, face-to-face instruction and support from dedicated and skilled teachers is considered to be an essential component of successful learning. The Framework for Action specifically addresses the need to:

— *Use distance, online, and virtual education as well as video-conferencing as strategic modes of delivering flexible individualised learning and training opportunities for young people in rural and remote areas;*

— *Provide affordable and accessible broadband Internet services for rural and remote locations;*

— *Expand and upgrade infrastructure and provide reliable technical support;*

— *Take advantage of opportunities for sharing ICT infrastructure, where appropriate;*

— *Ensure equitable access to quality online curriculum materials that are inclusive of rural and remote contexts and circumstances;*

— *Provide ICT training and development for staff; and*

— *Identify and share successful models of multimodal delivery.*

Teachers and principals in rural and remote schools face specific challenges including working with multi-age classes, increased administrative responsibilities, a high degree of graduate placement and teacher turnover, and adjusting to life in a geographically remote location. The Framework for Action specifically addresses the need to:

— *Improve recruitment and retention of teachers in rural and remote areas;*

— *Facilitate a two-way exchange between Education Queensland staff and local rural and remote communities;*

— *Recognise the differential workloads of principals and teachers in rural and remote schools and establish the right staffing mix to deliver high quality education services for rural and remote students;*

— *Provide support for systemic planning, administration and curriculum implementation in small schools, and*

— *Enhance rural and remote teachers ' access to relevant learning and development programs to ensure they are up to date in all areas of their work.*

To build community capacity and facilitate partnerships for creating innovative learning environments and efficient resourcing arrangements in rural and remote areas. The provision of quality education in rural and remote Queensland requires creative and flexible approaches that utilise leadership capacity at all levels, government and non-government collaboration, whole-of-district organising and community engagement.

It is acknowledged that the fundamental capacity of a rural or remote community to build and support learning environments will vary significantly throughout Queensland. The Framework for Action specifically addresses the need to:

- *Develop new models of collaboration and coordination across primary, secondary schools and training providers;*
- *Ensure equity and efficiency of resource allocation to best meet the needs of students in rural and remote schools;*
- *Take advantage of opportunities for sharing ICT infrastructure, where appropriate;*
- *Build partnerships between stakeholders from both within and among neighbouring communities so that effects caused through small populations are minimised;*
- *Increase community involvement to facilitate sustainability; and*
- *Enhance cooperation and integration to improve student pathways.*

Education Queensland will continue to trial New Basics in 2004 in 24 rural and remote schools. New Basics is an integrated framework of curriculum, pedagogy, assessment and reporting that aims to increase the proportion of Queensland students who complete Year 12 by reducing alienation in the middle years of schooling. The futures-oriented New Basics Curriculum is organised under four headings that cut across traditional disciplines: life pathways and social futures; multiliteracies and communications media; active citizenship; environment and technologies.

Education Queensland will continue to implement the Literate Futures project to ensure that all students develop the literacy skills they need to be successful in their school, work, social, civic and personal lives now and in the future. To date, all state schools have developed whole-school literacy strategies to improve student literacy outcomes. During 2003 -2005, schools will work to achieve improved outcomes for students and ensure that all teachers participate in learning and development programs on the teaching of reading.

Education Queensland will introduce the Middle Phase of Learning Core Curriculum project. This project will: Define the range, balance and continuity of learnings that will comprise the core curriculum in Years 4 -9; and Establish trials of clustered teachers developing sample work programs; 'Uncluttering ' the middle phase curriculum in state schools will provide more space and time for students to achieve deeper understanding and higher levels of engagement in learning. This will be accompanied by greater curriculum consistency across classrooms and schools, and greater continuity across year levels.

Education Queensland will continue to participate in a joint project with Queensland Health and Disability Services Queensland to establish a more coordinated approach to service provision for people with disabilities in Queensland. Initially, the project will focus on identifying issues and options for developing more coordinated approaches for the delivery of occupational therapy, physiotherapy and speech language pathology services. The project will examine current models of service delivery in the areas of Ipswich, Toowoomba and south-west Queensland.

Education Queensland will investigate the trialling of delivering online support services for students with disabilities who attend schools in remote areas that do not have ready access to local specialist teachers and specialist support personnel. This service will complement the visiting specialist support services that are provided to these schools. The trial would also explore the provision of online support services to students with disabilities who access their education at home through a School of Distance Education.

Education Queensland will trial the delivery of a

preparatory year in distance education in 2004. In 2003, the focus is on developing support materials for distance education teachers and home tutors to implement the draft Early Years Curriculum Guidelines.

Education Queensland will provide an option to students attending remote and very remote schools with highly modified curriculum to access Distance Education to facilitate them receiving a more appropriate curriculum. In some remote and very remote communities, the school's curriculum is modified in ways that best meet the educational needs and circumstances of the majority of children in that community - for example, the curriculum may be delivered in a language other than English.

All applications for Remote Curriculum Enhancement will be negotiated on a case-by-case basis through the local school principal. Students receiving this option will be entitled to the same standard of service provided to the geographically isolated category of distance education enrolment. The provision of distance education materials and teaching from a School of Distance Education will be provided free of charge and delivered to the student at and through their local state school.

Education Queensland will trial in 2004 coordination of secondary school offerings for Years 11 and 12 home-based geographically isolated learners through the Charters Towers School of Distance Education (SDE). This project will build on the school's existing partnerships with the local state high school, the Brisbane School of Distance Education, TAFE providers, registered training organisations and the Open Learning Institute to ensure there are appropriate local learning and training pathways for secondary students enrolled at the school.

The trial will enable the school to provide greater continuity, improved pastoral care and better access to a range of academic and vocational education programs that reflect student aspirations and regional employment opportunities. This trial may be expanded to other SDEs in 2005.

Education Queensland will continue to facilitate school-based apprenticeship and traineeship programs, which enable students to study for their Senior Certificate and, at the same time, undertake paid work and receive recognised training. Students in rural and remote regions who participate in school-based apprenticeships and traineeships have the opportunity to train in a wide range of industries that they might not otherwise be able to access.

Education Queensland will introduce, from 2004, an annual subsidy to assist geographically isolated distance education families to access broadband Internet services. It will also continue to influence the Commonwealth to provide ongoing affordable broadband Internet access to distance education students in rural and remote Queensland.

Distance Education Enhancement Project (DEEP)

Education Queensland will continue to roll out the Distance Education Enhancement Project, a package of reforms for distance education students in the geographically isolated and medical categories. This project ensures equity of access for distance education students living in rural and remote areas of Queensland and includes four interrelated components: digitisation of education materials; conversion of all Schools of Distance Education (SDEs) from HF radio to telephone teaching over 2003 and 2004; provision of an annual subsidy for computer-related hardware; and subsidising the costs of Internet downloads and data transfer in the home classroom.

SDEs will work closely with students, parents and school

communities to facilitate a successful transition to using digital materials and to tailor solutions to meet their individual needs and capacity. Education Queensland will, in 2004, deliver recommendations about expanding some aspects of the DEEP initiative to other distance education enrolment categories.

Education Queensland will continue to trial live data-conferencing lessons to distance education students in their homes.This online delivery mode increases student engagement with learning, enables intensive tutoring, and fosters teacher - student interactivity and student collaboration.

Education Queensland will trial the delivery of online curriculum to students in non-state school locations through the Virtual Schooling Service (VSS). Over the last three years, the VSS's i-school has delivered quality online education and increased the subject range available to over 750 Years 11 and 12 students attending small and/or rural and remote secondary state schools. Commencing in Term 3 2003, the trial of i-school in non-state school locations aims to:

Education Queensland will enhance and coordinate online education and VET provision to provide flexible learning pathways to meet the needs of 15 -17-year-olds who are most at risk of disengaging with school. The Virtual Schooling Service's i-support program will continue to provide online support and career education (including VET modules) for secondary students in rural and remote areas with limited access to guidance services.

Education Queensland will trial a cluster-based delivery of Virtual Schooling Service (VSS) technology to provide extracurricular programs for secondary students in bypassed schools. The VSS model offers bypassed schools the opportunity to establish cohorts of students in particular year levels across rural and remote sites. By delivering extracurricular online programs in areas such as career education and Music, students at bypass schools will gain access to broader subject offerings and participate in collaborative e-learning environments,and teachers will explore new models of curriculum delivery.

Education Queensland will investigate enhancing rural and remote teachers ' access to relevant learning and development programs. Education Queensland will facilitate rural and remote districts to develop online learning communities for teachers in rural and remote areas. These communities will deliver online learning and development and also enable teachers to connect with other teachers within their district and across the state to share innovative classroom strategies and best practice models in rural and remote education.

Basic Education for Rural People

Rural - urban disparities are issues of major concern for the international community and FAO member countries, as are disparities in education in rural areas. 70 percent of the world's poor live in rural areas, where children's access to education, adult literacy and quality education are still much lower than in urban areas.

In this regard, FAO and UNESCO are reaching out to key partners to join them in the following concern: if rural people do not have better access to basic education, the two Millennium Development Goals of poverty and hunger eradication and universal primary education will not be achieved by 2015.

While quality education is a right on its own, basic education is also one of the conditions for food security and sustainable development. This is why FAO and UNESCO are building a new partnership to support education for rural populations. The partnership, launched at the World Summit for

Sustainable Development (WSSD) in Johannesburg on September 3 2002, is a new flagship for a world-wide initiative on 'Education for All'.

The partnership is open to members committed to working individually or together to promote and facilitate basic quality education for rural populations. NGOs and other civil society organisations (under no financial obligation other than the one already undertaken through projects they promote in favour of basic education in rural areas) are invited to join FAO and UNESCO in a partnership designed to increase co-ordinated and collaborative efforts with and for rural populations.

Primary, Secondary and Vocational Education

Several NGOs focus their activities on expanding access to education, as they firmly believe that education enables people to improve their living conditions. In many countries however, governments are unable to provide rural people with sufficient and appropriate access to education.

Schools frequently undergo teacher and didactic material shortages, while the buildings are often small, dilapidated and unhygienic. NGOs work to provide adequate infrastructures to develop and maintain schools in remote rural areas. Another aspect the projects have in common is the linkage between school and agriculture.

Curriculas and programmes are often prepared for urban schools, then transferred without adaptation to rural areas. In most cases, the links between school and agriculture are overlooked, as are the economic, social and cultural needs of rural areas. As a response to parents requests for assistance in providing education, NGOs set-up a number of projects for their children, such as: agricultural education, literacy and numeracy.

Furthermore, according to ACRA, parents want their children to understand their cultural background, to feel a sense of belonging to their land, so that they will want to take care of it in the future. With this perspective in mind, school is not a 'waste of time', but an opportunity to learn how to read and write, and to apply theory to local agricultural and rural development needs.

Several NGO projects support schools that link education to agriculture, where in addition to literacy and numeracy, students have lessons in agriculture, breeding and horticulture. For example, in the afternoon, students spend time working in the school's orchard and vegetable garden, putting theoretical lessons into practice.

In Brazil, OPAM and AECOFABA (Associationes Escuela Familia Bahia) collaborate with a school called Agriculture Family School (part of the international movement of the "Maisons Rurales Familiales"), which has adopted a special approach: the 'rotation' of work and school. Students alternate 2 weeks of studying at school with 2 weeks of working at home, thereby ensuring that they are not totally separated from their natural habitat and family.

They spend three years studying practical and theoretical subjects, learning techniques on how to sow, cultivate, harvest, breed animals and keep bees. Consequently, when they return to their rural communities, they have a better understanding of agriculture and a higher sense of social awareness.

The development of school gardens is a frequent characteristic of many NGO projects, and essential for the promotion of pedagogic, economic, social and nutritional aspects. Besides linking the curriculum to the local environment, the gardens provide the opportunity for introducing students to new varieties of fruit and vegetables, thus improving their quality of nutrition. Moreover, by selling surplus products, the gardens generate a small income, which helps the school maintain itself and, in some cases, to survive.

Bilingual and Intercultural Education

An additional common aspect addressed by Italian NGOs, is intercultural and bilingual education. Very often teachers do not know the local language; school programs are developed in the official language of the country, and often do not adequately reflect local history and customs. Consequently, young people begin to reject their own language and culture. The methodology used is based on Mapuche indigenous culture, on the actual socio-economic conditions, on the prospects of integration in the school system, and in the local labour market.

ASIA has developed a cultural centre in rural China with a library of over 4000 volumes in Tibetan, Chinese and English. In 1995, in Chiapas (Mexico), MANI TESE and the local partner ZNLA started a secondary school project in rural areas with the aim of training bilingual teachers for primary schools.

The fight against the exploitation of child labour in rural areas is an issue dealt with by several NGOs. According to MANI TESE, the exploitation of child labour is inversely proportional to the increase in illiteracy. In India, MANI TESE and the local partner MGRES (Maria Grace Rural Education Society) not only work to provide education to rural working children, but also to sensitise parents to the importance of education and the serious consequences of child exploitation.

MANI TESE and MGRES train rural people in income-generating activities to develop financial independence; they also provide legal assistance to the victims of rights violations.

The AIFO example is particularly interesting because it promotes primary school education in rural India for children with disabilities. The AIFO and ST. JOSPEH SERVICE SOCIETY (local partner) project consists of a school where disabled children study alongside non-disabled children. The project aims at a multiplication effect , namely to facilitate rural disabled children's access to formal education.

Non Formal Education and Women's Rights

Different NGOs recognise the importance of addressing women's educational needs, especially for those living in rural areas. There are two issues which NGOs consider most important in rural areas: firstly, to increase women's awareness of their rights; secondly, to ensure that women obtain the essential education needed to ensure and promote their financial independence and wellbeing.

In many countries, and particularly in rural areas, women's rights are violated. Women suffer from abuse, brutality and marginalisation, which means that they are unable to fully participate in society. In Bangladesh, OPAM and Rural Vision (Social Voluntary Organization) have set up programs to address the needs of women and their husbands in 20 rural villages.

The goal is to provide information on women's rights and on equality between the sexes. As such, the project organises a social education course, which uses the following methods: documentaries on torture and violence against women are shown, and seminars with village leaders are held on both strengthening women's rights and reducing violence against women.

Literacy projects are numerous, and linked to the development of fundamental life skills. Often these are basic agricultural skills, which provide technical knowledge to support crop cultivation. These basic skills help to produce the types of food needed for a balanced diet, thus linking agricultural education to nutrition.

Literacy projects are also connected to health education in the subsequent ways: the development of basic skills related to improving hygiene conditions, monitoring the growth of children, preventing HIV/AIDS and treating the most common illnesses. Further, many NGOs firmly believe in the concept of providing women with basic income-generating skills, which promote economic independence.

Consequently, courses are provided in a variety of disciplines, such as: tailoring, dressmaking, sewing, the breeding of small animals, the cultivating of medicinal plants and spices, handicrafts and small and micro enterprises.

Regarding projects related to non-formal education for the population in general, once again the most important goals were: literacy and numeracy; agricultural education; nutrition and health education; small and micro enterprises. Some interesting specific aspects were analysed: ADRA and the local partners Adventist Development Relief Agency Philippines and Mountain View College, have a school project in the Philippines, where parents and children are in the same class; they study the same subjects and they complement their studies with musical education.

It was proved that children learn faster than their parents do, and that they participate more actively in social activities. ISCOS uses a technical training method based on adult education; the method follows a circular path: theory-practice-verification-theory. By linking theory and practice, they were able to provide employment for people in areas that required their newly learned skills, allowing them to see the results of their education immediately.

In the early 1990s, a project in health education aimed at preventing HIV in Zambia. The project addressed young people of school age. It included sex education lessons for students, and training courses in sex education for local teachers.

The project was deemed a success, and as Zambia is one of the countries most affected by the HIV virus, sex education lessons were extended to younger students, while training courses were expanded to street educators in order to reach those who have dropped out of school.

Several non-formal education projects are run by "Para-teachers" who produce excellent results. This fact confirms the hypothesis that a teacher's motivation can, to a certain extent, compensate for a lack of formal teacher training and qualifications. An interesting common aspect is the safeguarding of the environment. Training and educational projects promote sustainable agriculture, soil control, water preservation, and careful energy use.

Some NGOs develop the practise of IPM (Integrated Pest Management), as does FAO, discouraging the use of destructive pesticides and expensive fertilisers, while encouraging the use of organic products. An additional common aspect is the development of associations or farmers' co-operatives. The aim is to take advantage of co-operatives in order to increase productivity. Often, a co-operative has more purchasing power in the market or with suppliers, and can easily obtain credit from Banks or financial entities.

In addition, a co-operative can provide its members with a technical assistance centre or practical professional training courses. In Senegal, ISCOS and CNTS, have created self-sustaining bread-making co-operatives, capable of producing high quality mixed-grain bread at a fair price. In Lebanon, ICU has developed an important project for a farmer's co-operative, which focuses on the following aspects:

- — *The quality control of olive oil (the program has established oil analysis equipment and facilities, and performs oil analysis services for farmers and oil mills).*
- — *A distribution program of selected fruit trees to improve quality and quantity output of fruit farms.*

Primary Education

In 1979, the outbreak of civil war in Chad (Latin America) led to the closure of many primary schools and a reduction in the number of trained teachers; this resulted in the overcrowding of the few village schools that remained open. With the school-age population increasing, the state has been unable to provide schooling for those who need it. Schooling, the community and agriculture are primarily considered separate entities in Chad.

Specifically, cultural prejudices counter the concept of education, as schooling is seen as merely a way of training civil servants. The population in Guerà reacted to the lack of primary schools in Chad by setting-up an organization called "The Association of Parents of Students". The Association pays teachers' salaries and builds schools through self-taxation.

The aim of the association is to educate children by linking the school to agriculture. Parents want their children to know about their roots, to feel a sense of belonging to their land, and to ensure the land is cared for in the future. With this perspective, school is no longer considered a "waste of time", but an occasion to learn how to write and read, and to apply theory to local agricultural needs.

Teachers on the other hand, provided the didactic material, collected and printed several local stories, myths, and tales, wrote them in the local dialect and translated them into French. In order to connect literacy to agriculture, the students spend three hours in the afternoon on practical lessons in the school's orchard and vegetable garden. They learn and put into practice improved horticulture and agriculture methods. Parents are also involved in showing students practical agricultural techniques and an expert teacher supervises all the agricultural activities.

Tchirimina Village, in the Atacora' region in Benin, is classified as a district of the urban area of Natitingou. The Tchirimina area was originally a forest situated at the base of a mountain, but the population has increased so quickly in recent years, that many ethnic groups such as the Wama, Otamari, Dindi, Bariba, Yoruba, Natimba, Fon e Peul now live there.

The 6000 inhabitants in the village base their subsistence on handicrafts and small businesses, but the main activity is still agriculture. Tchirimina Elementary School was built in 1982. In 1997, school attendance increased to 544 students and with US funding, the village was able to build three more classrooms. The school also uses three rented classrooms, but these are completely unsuitable for teaching.

In general terms, the quality of school education is low in the indigenous rural areas of Chile. Schools are beset with a number of serious problems, for example: the few existing classrooms are crumbling, there are few pedagogical and didactic tools available, there is often no heating or electricity, and school lunches are frequently prepared in unhygienic conditions.

The school also faces the problem of coping with the lack of a suitable bilingual teaching (Mapudungun - Spanish). The majority of the children go to school speaking their maternal language (Mapudungun), whilst their teachers only speak Spanish. From the language, to the contents of teaching, everything is based on the negation of Mapuche identity and culture. This creates a divide in the mind of the child who starts refusing his own language and culture.

In this situation, it is not unusual to see a decrease in the number of pupils attending school in the Maquehue territory. Pupils, who are expected to take an active part in agricultural and domestic tasks at home, cannot always attend school. Scarcer still is the percentage of young people who decide to continue their studies. To cope with this situation, the project has worked with teachers to develop a study on the linguistic characteristics of the pupils.

There is a strong reluctance however, to recognize the bilingual situation, and to adjust school programs to encompass Mapuche identity and culture - essential factors that must be recognized in order to improve the children's learning skills.

Community Service Agents

This is a program of methodological support and production of teaching materials for adult education courses (women, young people). Students are chosen by their communities and are coordinated by the executives of their respective community organizations, who also assume an active and dynamic role in finding work for them.

Community Service Agents are also able to respond to specific needs, such as: assistance with health emergencies, repairing equipment, checking the quality of seeds, administering funds, managing contacts with institutions, etc. This activity has resulted in the creation of new jobs.

Rural Sanitary Agents (RSAs)

The program foresees the development of continuous education programmes for social-health operators (physicians, professional nurses, midwives, social assistants, nutritionists and rural nurses) working in the institutions operating in Maquehue. The contents are built through contacts with the local reality and the development of the practical activities of the RSAs.

The village of Dongche lies in Guide County, a rural area of Qinghai Province, Hainan Prefecture. The Administration (in Chinese Shan) covers an area of 60 sqKm. and is composed of eight so-called natural villages. Dongche is 20 Km. from Guide. ASIA has been working in this area since 1993 to improve the educational and cultural conditions of the local population.

In September 1997, a classes started up at a newly established Tibetan boarding school for 500 children. A cultural center with a library of over 4000 volumes in Tibetan, Chinese and English was also created. The school has 12 classrooms, dormitories for 120 nomad children, 22 lodgings for teachers, kitchens, bathrooms and storerooms. It was created with the objective of guaranteeing basic quality education to all the Tibetan village children, thus supplying them with the necessary instruments with which to uphold and spread the Tibetan language and culture.

The children of the Dongche Tibetan Primary School benefit from project activities together with the children of the surrounding nomadic families who find accommodation and living facilities at the school building. However the poorest families of this area, especially those who live too far away and would have to pay the expenses of board and lodging, are still unable to send their children to school.

For this reason, ASIA's Adoption at Distance Project selected these children to be adopted at distance, enabling them to attend school. The school is also used as a cultural, educational, and adult training centre to develop English and computer skills. A petrol pump for Dongche Tibetan Primary school was and is now operational.

Income from the pump will be given to the school to help the poorest families send their children to school, to improve the school conditions, and to organize teacher-training courses in school during holiday periods. These courses will include English, computer skills and pedagogic subjects. Funds for the building of the petrol pump were advanced by the local bank, hence ASIA is looking for a sponsor to bear the expenses of this initiative.

In 1998, a training program in English, computer science and the Tibetan language was set up. The training program was financed by IFAD from 1998 to 2000, and by ASIA for the year 2001. From 1998 to 2001, the project provided training for more than 200 teachers, and 250 children and adults. The necessary equipment for an information technology classroom and an English language laboratory (computers, scanners, photocopy machines, fax machines, tape recorders) was also provided. This project has enabled Tibetan teachers to become trainers for other teachers, and has provided them with skills and knowledge to pass on to their students.

As well as supporting the economic and social development of the Tibetan minority in the Hainan Prefecture, the courses have proven to be effective tools for empowerment. Consequently, the Department of Education and local communities of the Hainan Prefecture have requested ASIA to expand these training programs, and a project proposal is already being prepared by ASIA for a five-year plan for English and computer teacher training in Dongche.

Tamil Nadu, the state in which the Venkatayapuram region is found, is situated in the south of India. It contains 55 million inhabitants - 20% are out-casts and 60% are under-privileged. Despite the fact that Tamil Nadu is one of the most industrialized states in India, it contends with a number of serious problems, such as: the scourge of child labor, the exploitation of woman, the dowry, and the still existing caste system.

MGRES (Maria Grace Rural Education Society), a local NGO, and Mani Tese set-up a project to address the needs of the Dalit - the outcast rural population. The Dalit, agricultural workers with no land, are dependent on superior castes, who take advantage of their poverty and ignorance.

Dry weather in the area limits agricultural activity to only three months of the year, leaving families with insufficient means to support themselves for the remainder of the year. Consequently, people migrate to cities in the hope of finding better work opportunities. However, this is often a bad choice, asthey run into debt in order to survive, and are forced to become slaves to moneylenders. Their perceived "impurity" prevents them from leading a normal social life, and their inferiority is confirmed at every moment of their lives.

Poor living condition, malnutrition and meager immune defenses make them victims of contagious illnesses, and sick people are abandoned to the mercy of fate and to superstitious practices. Even nowadays, 60% of births take place at home, with a high risk of infections. The condition of women is desperate: society considers them inferior beings, and condemns them to a sub-human existence. Driven by these difficult living conditions, families are forced to send their children out to work in order to earn extra income.

Many children work as farm-laborers for tobacco companies and in cattle breeding. This results in both the exploitation of children, and an increase in the illiteracy rate. MGRES and Mani Tese launched a project aimed at informing the Dalit about their rights and improving their economic conditions. The project was set up in 22 villages and involved

1150 adults, 1089 children and 18 trainers. It has provided 50 training courses, 6 legal assistance campaigns and 6 health campaigns.

The training courses include health education, legal education, activities related to managing savings and to producing income, cultural activities and women's groups. The school offers two different courses: a pre-school 'first step towards education' course for children from ages 3 to 5 during the morning, , and a course for school-age children with the aim of providing remedial lessons and study groups during the afternoon.

Dzamthog village, located on the right bank of the Yangtse River, has traditionally been an agricultural area. Wheat, barley and potatoes are the main agricultural products grown by the local people, as the area has a good growing climate. The domestic economy of the villagers is completed by animal husbandry and forestry activities. Women dedicate their duties to agriculture. Dzamthog village is the center of an integrated development project implemented by ASIA, and financed by the Italian Government, with additional contributions from the Embassies of The Netherlands, Finland and France located in Beijing. The project has constructed and developed a district hospital, which utilizes both allopathic and traditional Tibetan medicine, and a Tibetan Primary School for 400 children.

ASIA has also constructed a new building for the school, which provides accommodation for 120 students. In 1996, the Jomda County Government donated 4 hectares of land to the project, which was leveled into different terraces and then prepared for cultivation. An extension of the existing irrigation system was also constructed, making the land more irrigable and the crops more plentiful and profitable.

Four greenhouses have also been built, increasing the

cultivation of vegetables and making it possible for teachers and doctors to transport vegetables from Dzamthog, without having to go to Derge, which is 25 km away. Part of the irrigable land was used for the creation of an apple tree orchard. Apple trees grow with good results in almost all the gardens in Gamthog village. A small tractor was purchased to facilitate agricultural work, and to transport products to the market in Dege.

Vocational training courses in agriculture for the local people are being carried out on the land, providing agricultural skills for the students from the Dzamthog School. All of the activities were carried out with the co-operation of the people of Dzamthog village. This project has given the school and clinic the opportunity to generate income through land cultivation, with the aim of increasing and sustaining access to primary education for Tibetan children from the area. The use of vegetables and fruit is not included in the traditional daily diet of Tibetans, but this habit is changing. Nowadays fruit is greatly appreciated by Tibetan children.

The State (region) of Bahia, in the north east of Brazil, is classified as a poor rural area. The economy is mainly based on agriculture, but also on chemical, petroleum and pharmacological industries. In recent years, public authorities have planned development projects for cities, with little investment in rural areas. Despite the fact that the farmer is the "back-bone" of Brazil, he still feels left out of the country's development programs.

This results in the migration of rural people to the city in the hope of finding a better life. AECOFABA (Associationes Escuela Familia Bahia), assisted by O.P.A.M. and the Italian Ministry of Foreign Affairs, gives support to the "Family Schools" project in the State of Bahia. AECOFABA is a civil association, founded in 1979, which takes the lead in supporting approximately 30 family schools. The project manages and co-

ordinates school programs, enrolls teachers and guarantees didactic materials.

The Government in Brazil only makes provisions for the first four years of a child's education. The Family School gives farmers' children the opportunity to study in an economically affordable situation and the Government legally recognizes the school. The Family School represents a home, school and community. Its aim is to educate youngsters to follow the customs and culture of their family and community. The schools are always located in rural areas and accept young farmers from different parts of the country.

The Family School's special approach is the "rotation" of work and school. Students alternatively spend 2 weeks studying at school and 2 weeks working in their home, thus ensuring that they are not totally separated from their natural habitat and family. The rotation of school and home benefits families, as youngsters can continue to help their families with household chores and daily duties. Schools also benefit, as the rotation of home and school ensures that a large number of students are able to be trained.

Students spend three years studying practical and theoretical subjects. When they return to their rural communities they have a good knowledge of agriculture and social issues. The school curriculum includes humanist science, mathematics and agricultural matters. During the afternoon, students spend three hours on theoretical lessons in the school's orchard and vegetable garden. There, they learn various techniques, such as: how to sow, cultivate, harvest, breed small animals and bee keeping.

A priority of the school is to encourage sustainable agriculture and the conservation of the environment and natural resources. The students study soil control, water preservation and careful energy use. The school also makes use of the goods they produce to feed students, buying only extra provisions required at the local market. At the end of each two-week school session, the cost of purchased goods is calculated and divided between the students. This sum is the only amount the students have to pay for their schooling.

The Merano Missionary Group has been active in western Africa for 30 years. The Organization works on structural projects (e.g., boring wells, catchment basins) and professional training projects. One of its projects has undertaken the planning and implementing of four domestic management training centers for women in Benin (Bohicon, Paracou, Bembereke) and Burkina Faso (Koudougou).

The program develops methodologies to improve knowledge in the fields of nutrition and health (especially for children), nutrition self-sufficiency and the sale of agricultural products. It also provides courses in dressmaking, cooking, kitchen gardening and the breeding of small animals. The duration of the whole training period is four years, but a certificate of attendance is provided after three.

The training centers survive thanks to the agricultural production provided by the students. A very important aspect of the program is the provision of clean water from wells, established by the Merano Missionary Group during the past 30 years. One of the main activities of the Group is the boring of wells in different pre-Sahelian areas (more than 500 to date), and the establishment of teaching centers for the local population.

The Group also provides training courses for girls on the use of clean water from wells. The aim is the dissemination of information to the population on the need to request the construction of wells and catchment basins. At the end of the course, the girls go back to their villages and use their skills in hygiene, agriculture, small trade and handicrafts.

The Monze district, in Zambia, is a region with no industrial development and poor agricultural conditions; therefore, agriculture cannot guarantee sufficient welfare and employment for the local population. An agricultural school for young people in order to provide them with the qualified and specialized skills needed to improve agricultural production in the area.

The project consists of two stages. The first is a theoretical course aimed at teaching young people new techniques on agriculture and breeding. The second is a concrete course, which puts the theoretical lessons into practice. The courses have resulted in the development of a production unit by the students. The unit is used as a sample to develop private units for students, and ensures economic support for the school's activity. Thirty students participate in the course every year.

The school teaching supports sustainable agriculture and includes: horticulture, the control of fungiform pathologies, and damage caused by insects; the breeding of bovines, hogs, goats and chickens, the anatomy and pathology of animals; the prevention and care of animal illness, techniques for soil care and erosion; the methodology of storage, bookkeeping and techniques for crop selling.

The project lasts three years, after which the population is expected to continue the activity started during the course under the supervision of the Diocese of Monze. The project is based in Assam State, in the Northeastern part of India. One of the major activities of the project is to give assistance to tribal people who are exploited by local money-lenders.

When tribal people receive small loans for the lands mortgaged, money-lenders take the greater part of their crop. Once people fall into the trap, they are not able to redeem the mortgaged land. Poor education facilities and inaccessible schools create another serious problem in the area. School attendance is very low, with high rates of illiteracy and school dropouts. In the project area, the main health problems are linked to endemic diseases like malaria and tuberculosis, while the under-five mortality rate is very high due to diarrhoea and malnutrition. The project works through the establishment of Self-Help Groups (SHGs) in the tribal villages.

Educational coaching centers have been established in the tribal villages. These centers are managed by trained local personnel (coaching persons), selected by the villagers. Their function is to organize after-school support lessons, to monitor the regular presence of teachers and to support the teaching procedures in the villages' Government schools. The project also supports two schools, one in Manikbond with 255 students, and the second one in a village with 40 students. 20 coaching centres are active in the villages, providing equal opportunities for education to more than 600 children.

The project's target area now covers 30 villages. Currently, there are 75 functioning SHGs. Since 1998, a total of 280 acres of mortgaged land has been redeemed from money-lenders (with a 50% contribution from SHGs members), and 429 persons have benefited. With regards to health care, activities include awareness-raising about disease prevention activities (informal meetings and training courses on the basic principles of Primary Health Care and the role of traditional medicine) in order to reduce the mortality rates among children under five years of age.

The project is also planning to start community-based rehabilitation activities for children and adults with disabilities living in the area. The Mexican constitution guarantees local people the right to fully develop their indigenous culture and to organize their lives freely. In 1995, MANI TESE started a secondary school project with the aim of training bilingual teachers for primary schools. MANI TESE started building the school in 1996. It now contains 4 classrooms , two dormitories, a refectory and kitchen, and a large library with books donated from all over the world. The students, nearly 200 males and females, are chosen from among the best primary school pupils.

Those who come from the country live at the school, while their families provide their food (beans and tortillas). The project provides not only theoretical studies but also practical experience in every day life and work. "Rural Vision" is a Christian social voluntary organization for human development in Bangladesh. Its aim is to promote the socio-economic and cultural development and dignity of the rural underprivileged, especially the poorest people of Khulna and Satkira Districts. In these districts, education and literacy rates are low: male 33.2% and female 17.6%. There is a lack of awareness on the importance of education, which has thus contributed to the low literacy rate, increased polygamy, divorce, early marriage and physical humiliation.

The Director of Rural Vision, set-up five pre-schools in rural villages, in which 150 children are taught every year. After three years, the children are admitted to the local primary school. Five centers were set-up, one per village. The pre-education center of each village is located in a rented house with sufficient space for learners, facilities for play areas, safe drinking water and sanitation. Village people are directly involved in the development process to increase the success of the project.

Before starting work, qualified teachers who are chosen to work in the centers attend a 12-day training course on: child education, pedagogy, psychology, teaching learning/methods, monitoring and reporting. During the school program, teachers attend an additional 3-day intensive course to strengthen and improve their teaching methods. Each teacher is responsible for a class of 30 children. Literacy and numeracy are taught along with family welfare. Classes are held for 3 hours on a daily basis, 5 days a week. The program lasts 12 months. A literacy test is taken every 4 months and a certificate is provided to the students after their final examination.

Zambia has one the highest rates of HIV infection in the world; the virus infects approximately 20% of the population. The illness primarily affects young people, and causes devastating social and economic conditions. Due to the diffusion of HIV, expenses for health services are increasing and the labor supply is decreasing. After the first case of HIV, in the mid-1980s, the government launched a direct information and sensitization campaign, but the results were not successful.

Ce.L.I.M. launched a project aimed at preventing HIV, in the Siavonga district, at the beginning of the 1990s. The project started in collaboration with some local schools and addressed young people of school age. The program included sex education lessons for students and training courses in sex education for local teachers. The project was so successful that the Education Ministry and Diocese of Monze asked Ce.L.I.M. to strengthen and extend the program.

Ce.L.I.M.'s new project includes sex education lessons for even younger students, and training courses to street educators for school drop-outs. The project foresees the education of a supervisor, eight courses in local schools; training courses for four school educators; and courses for 20 street educators.

The territory of Huilio in the IX region of Chile, is inhabited by the Mapuches, an indigenous community. The Mapuches represent approximately 10% of the population of

Chile. They live in conditions of extreme poverty and suffer the consequences of political decisions, which repress small-scale agriculture and do nothing to actively sustain the cultural and social codes of ethnic minorities.

The project proposed the improvement of the social and economic conditions and the quality of life of the Mapuche communities, by giving importance to Mapuche culture as a resource for the process of modernization. The project's activities regarding basic rural education were aimed at farming families. The main activity gave priority to the involvement of youth; the sector that is most likely to emigrate to the city to compensate for the lack of local opportunities.

Particular attention was given to women, whose productive role is valued within traditional culture. The training activities for production were aimed at the following sectors: administration, production, and activities for the transformation and marketing of agricultural products, management of credits and the design of productive micro-projects. From this process, two productive micro projects were developed: apiculture and biological agriculture.

The Mapuche farmers recognized the existence of real possibilities for the development of this type of agriculture, which respects the natural environment, and maintains traditional Mapuche culture and food. The apiculture micro project was preceded by theoretical and practical training, which included the division of responsibility for the management of a collective educational beehive, the preparation of the substance for harvesting, and its transformation into honey.

A literacy and numeracy activity was developed using Intercultural & Bilingual Education (IBE) methodology: education through schooling is the frontier between the process of education and integration into the national society. The IBE involves the elders, depositaries of traditional knowledge and the younger generations, who represent modernization.

The language, practices and traditional concepts, considered useless by western society, were revalued in order to achieve better didactic results. The project developed a refresher program for teachers through "lesson types" developed in the classroom, contacts within the community through the organization of traditional cultural events and the elaboration of didactic materials.

The Liberation Movement for Women (LMW)

The Liberation Movement for Women (LMW) was legally constituted 12 years ago and has been working for the social development, participation and empowerment of women at the grass roots level in 50 different Indian communities ever since. In India, where women are exploited within the community, Dalit women suffer the most.

Due to insufficient rainfall, rural Dalit people are forced to migrate from place to place in order to survive, thus increasing illiteracy and child labor. Female education is not at all encouraged, and as a consequence many girls become prey to early marriage, unmarried motherhood and prostitution.

In order to improve the situation for these girls and to provide them with a better future, LMW decided to implement a special coaching program for young Dalit girls. Due to the circumstances described above, many Dalit girls fail their secondary level public examination and become dropouts. LMW developed the following project to enable these girls to become masters of their own destinies through education.

Every year, 60 girls (divided into two groups, starting at different timeperiods) are selected for a training and coaching program, which lasts 5 months and will prepare them for the secondary level government examination.These skills will provide the girls with better qualifications and increase their future opportunities.

With the repatriation of the population, two essential needs had to be taken into immediate consideration: the re-establishment of basic services and the development of economic activities. Throughout the 1994/95 period, efforts were mainly concentrated on the re-establishment of basic services. CIES worked in the District capital, Espungabera, and in the central District areas in close cooperation with the local authorities, International Agencies and National and International NGOs operating in the Province.

Within such poor communities, the status of women is particularly precarious. They lack access to productive resources and their income-earning possibilities areminimal. In spite of this, women are active in handicrafts, sewing, food processing and small trade. One activity is the tailoring of traditional Tibetan dresses, which are used during weddings and other important ceremonies.

Increasing demand from the expanding tourist sector has created an additional market stimulus. Traditional Tibetan dress-making requires a specific know-how, which at present is retained by elderly women. However, the safeguarding and further development of this type of manual art are threatened, as younger generations of women face a number of problems when setting-up a tailoring business.

The project on the promotion of women tailoring groups has just started and aims at safeguarding and expanding this traditional knowledge through training and promoting investments in traditional and other dress-making activities for the market. The project supports two groups of women in setting up income generating activities in tailoring. While, the groups specialize in traditional Tibetan dress and garment making, they also produce modern dresses and carry out darning and mending work.

As most of the women were illiterate, some literate daughters, interested in learning the tailoring of traditional garments, were co-opted to fulfill the functions of treasurer and secretary of the group. The project is managed by a Nepalese non-governmental organization called Women Acting Together for CHange (WATCH), based in Kathmandu. WATCH is a Resource-support organization (RSO), which means that its main role is to train and strengthen other smaller non-governmental organizations and grass-root groups.

The project activities are carried out in the following three rural areas: an area in the high mountains called Okhaldunga; an area near the national capital Katmandu, called Chaimalle; and finally an area in the low plains or the Terai region, called Rupendehi. In each project area, the activities include: the promotion of women groups through participatory methodologies and creating a federation of these groups, training village volunteers for community health services, promoting informal adult education classes, promoting social forestry groups, reclaiming forest lands, and promoting seed-funds and credit funds for income generation activities, etc.

All of the project's activities are focused on women from lower castes and tribal groups, who are usually the poorest people in villages. Some activities, like creating groups for channeling and using common water, veterinary service groups etc. also involve men. At present there are 70 women's groups in the project areas, who have formed a national federation together. They act locally to deal with problems like AIDS, women-trafficking in neighbouring India, the sexual exploitation of women and children, etc. They also act nationally, pushing for changes to national policies and laws.

In Bangladesh 12 percent of women are literate, whilst the percentage of literate men is 26 percent. Women are socially handicapped. Despite the fact that they have the same civil rights as men, in reality, society considers them inferior beings, the property of males, and condemns them to a sub-human level of life. This situation has existed for centuries and is not easy to change. Two of the most important factors required to bring about change in women's lives are literacy and economic independence.

In these schools, women are trained in literacy, health and hygiene and basic financial literacy. They receive technical support for homestead vegetable cultivation and lessons on nutrition. At the end of the course, the learners take a non-formal test. Women who complete the program will be expected to be able to read and write in their language (Bengali).

In Bangladesh, women are often victims of torture, violence and injustice. They are unaware of their rights and unable to protest when these rights are violated. If women are not educated about their rights, they cannot be expected to fully participate in society. For these reasons, O.P.A.M, in co-operation with the Ratandia Unnayan Sangstha (RUS), launched an annual program for 1000 women and their husbands. The aim is to develop awareness on women's rights, male-female differences, and the practice of torture and violence against women.

This project will start in 20 rural villages and will be conducted by the village trainers. During the training period, participants will learn about the conceptual framework of gender relationships, gender gaps, women's rights and male-female differences. The project shows films focused on violence against women, hands out posters on women's torture and violence, holds seminars with village leaders and religious leaders on the abuse of power against women, and arranges for at least two protest processions against injustice.

India grows 8.000 known medicinal plants and one third can be found in the Tamil Nadu and Kerala regions. More than 800 of them are in used in the Indian Medical System, whilemany others are used for homemade remedies or as food integrators. About 90 percent of the medicinal plant supplies are taken from the existing forests, causing a serious threat to conservation.

Although no systematic estimates of the threat status of medicinal plants has been carried out, rapid appraisals have shown that at least 250 species are threatened in India, half of them in the mentioned regions. The increasing request for medicinal plant supplies, both from the local and external market, while being a matter of concern for the species survival, is being considered by local NGO's as an income-generating opportunity for villagers who are located in areas where such plants could be cultivated.

The present market situation of medicinal plants is unregulated and difficult to access. The traders of quality plants for the pharmaceutical industry are few, and the cultivators-collectors disorganized. At the village-level, middlemen favor low-costs against quality. Increasing requests from the international market are presently not stable, but it is becoming clear that the main focus for the medicinal plants industry will be quality, proper cultivation/processing techniques, in a clean environment by organic means.

However, women are not in a position to take the lead in the development processes in India; therefore, an additional effort must be made to involve them at all levels, from production to processing to marketing. The group approach to women's involvement has, in the last few years, been the most efficient and effective way to support women's empowerment and their active role in development.

Women are mobilized in Self-help Groups (SHG), which are then provided with credit and technical inputs to undertake economic activities. The group provides a base for self-employment and empowerment through group dynamics.

In Salvador the health and hygiene conditions of children are appalling, Typhus, cholera, hepatitis and gastroenteritis are frequent illnesses, while malnutrition and hunger are serious problems. All over Africa, the condition of women is desperate. Most young girls are illiterate because from an early age, they are expected to work for the family with tasks such as carrying water, gathering firewood and minding their siblings.

Through literacy, women learn human rights and democracy practices. With the aim of preventing malnutrition through correct nutrition. This course teaches how to keep a kitchen garden and promotes a variety of food and a well-balanced diet. The school's aim is to help women find their roles and enables them to integrate into society.

Bulo, in Uganda, is a rural village located 80 miles from Kampala. The civil war in the late 1980s, and the current HIV crisis have affected a large number of men in the village. Consequently, women have had to assume the role of the heads of the family. In the last two decades, overpopulation and development in the Philippines have placed considerable pressure on the culture and the environment of the tribal population of Mindanao. One of the most affected tribes is the "Manobo", natives from central Mindanao.

Consequently, the tribal people have expressed a desire to learn ways of improving their living conditions, to learn technologies in agriculture, to read, write and count. Both adults and children attended the same classes. The education program involved many activities; for example, adults and children learned how to read and write in the tribal dialect, in the main local language as well as in English. They learned how to count and recognize peso bills or coins, in order to be able to trade with the people in the city.

The idea of teaching both adults and children had positive results. It was proved that children learned faster than their parents did and participated more actively in demonstrating activities. Children also learned to sing and to play instruments, as musical abilities were developed through the initiatives of the teachers. Children were invited to put on shows to demonstrate their talent at important community programs everywhere in the Province.

The Primary Health Care Program operated in the 22 villages and 292 mothers attended the health classes. The program aimed at improving the health status of women, children and the whole community through the dissemination of information. The relationship between hygiene and health was taught, stressing the importance of improving hygienic conditions by bathing, washing clothes and using clean water. The importance of food nutrition and cooking was underlined, as well as cleanliness in cooking areas. Training included the study of common illnesses such as cough, fever, ear-infections, wounds, and scabies; it also included preventive health care in immunization, breastfeeding and growth monitoring.

Alternative medicine (the use of herbal medication) was introduced to all centers. The villagers were taught the proper use and dosage of herbal medicine. These herbal plants grow easily in any type of soil, therefore, they are readily available, and have fewer side effects than medicines sold in pharmacies. The aim was to promote sustainable agriculture techniques that discourage the use of destructive pesticides and expensive fertilizers, and encourage the use of organic products, soil control and appropriate farm management techniques. The villagers were introduced to IPM (Integrated Pest Management), a technique that taught farmers to reduce the use of pesticides and turn to organic cultivation.

One of the most important consequences of the recent war in Kosovo, was that 75 percent of the rural population migrated: 43 percent fled abroad and 32 percent was scattered all over the country. Nowadays, 85 percent of these families have returned to their own villages. As a consequence of the war, agricultural production decreased, the harvest in 1999 was approximately 45 percent that of the one in 1997, agricultural tools used by farmers were seriously damaged, while seed, fertilizer and gasoline supplies were poor.

The program has undertaken research on the oil industry situation in the Southern Mount Lebanon area and has defined needs and priorities for modernisation. In the implementation phase, the participating industries present investment plans which are evaluated by a project management. If the evaluation is positive, they are awarded grants totalling up to 50 percent of the investment a program for quality control of olive oil. The program has established oil analysis facilities, and equipment and performs oil analysis services, for farmers and oil mills.

2

Communication and Rural Education Enhancement

A strong relationship between education and economic competitiveness is generally accepted at the national level, and concerns over continued economic growth have provided the primary motivation for the school reform movement. Education is viewed as equally important in writings specific to the South. Education is considered the primary vehicle for improving regional economic performance.

In particular, rural areas in the South are viewed as being in a period of transition, a period in which the education and skill levels of the labor force are becoming increasingly critical to the welfare of rural residents and rural communities. National and international market forces continue to erode the competitive position of traditional rural industries while the forces of deregulation and structural shifts within the national economy are tending to further concentrate economic activity in metropolitan areas.

At the same time, structural change within agriculture further reduces the number of jobs while modernization of traditional manufacturing industry and the emergency of technology oriented industries mean higher education requirements for most jobs. In short, a number of sources stress the importance of an educated, skilled workforce to the future of the South and call for increased development of the region's human capital.

Clearly, education is strongly related to economic growth. However, when the term "development" is used in a broader sense to refer to economic vitality or capacity building, education is more paramount. This approach focuses on the broader concepts of development and raises issues such as entrepreneurship, adaptability, innovation, and local control-all areas in which human capital plays a crucial role in success.

However, aside from the number of reports stressing the general importance of education to development, there is little in the way of an empirical foundation to support specific investments in improving education. Few seem to doubt that evident declines in productivity growth at the national level are linked to declines in school performance, but there has been little analysis of how school reform influences productivity growth.

At the regional or community level, the relationship between educational improvements and economic growth is less clear, and there is ample reason to suspect that the strength of the relationship is easily overstated. It is not clear that increased investment will result in educational improvements, and it is also not clear as to how (or if) such efforts translate to economic improvement.

Building on human capital theory, researchers have looked extensively at questions of school/student performance, at the role of communities and families in the educational process, and at relationships between expenditures and school outcomes. Much of the educational research in various disciplines, including education, is subject to the criticisms of being general in nature, of containing an urban bias, and being of limited usefulness to the rural policy makers.

For example, Levin notes that, "economic research on education is often viewed as exotic, arcane, and outside of the mainstream of what is normally viewed as educational research," and Hobbs notes the tendency for education policy to be based on "beliefs" rather than empirically supported conclusions about education. He notes the beliefs that large schools are more effective and efficient, that schools alone are responsible for educational outcomes, and that test scores are a good measure of education and can be used to judge the quality of schools.

Perhaps the most useful starting point for rural education research is to focus on increasing the available information on rural schools. There is, for example, a National Rural Education Association and a Southern Rural Education Association; there are a number of centers in colleges of education which focus specifically on problems of rural schools; and there are rural education programs in the Regional Educational Laboratories. This perception of differences is supported by the work of Bender et al. which attests to the economic and social diversity among nonmetropolitan counties.

There is, however, little hard evidence on how rural schools differ from their urban counterparts or on how rural schools are impacted by economic and social differences between rural and urban areas or by differences among rural areas. The call by Stevens for a meaningful taxonomy of rural schools would seem to be a useful starting point. He notes the tendency in policy circles to speak of education in general or simply of rural education, practices which do not account for rural-urban differences and which blur distinctions between rural areas in different parts of the county.

Stevens suggests a taxonomy of urban, suburban, and rural schools which includes context indicators (characteristics of the school district and community), input indicators (characteristics of students, staff, and fiscal inputs), process indicators (programs, leadership, etc.), and outcome indicators (both positive and negative). Stevens acknowledges the difficulty of his suggestion with reference to the size of the school enterprise in the United States.

Nationally, there are more than 15,000 school districts serving more than 40 million students. More than 3,000 school districts (21 percent of the U.S. total) are in the Southern states. Together, Southern states operate more than 24,000 separate schools serving more than 13 million students (33 percent of U.S. total). Four Southern states (Florida, Georgia, North Carolina and Texas) are among the ten largest state school systems in the country.

The smallest Southern state in terms of enrollment (Arkansas) has over 435 thousand students and ranks 33 in enrollment among the fifty states. In 1989-90 more than 734 thousand students graduated from high school in the South. Beyond numbers of schools and school districts, efforts to collect data on the socioeconomic characteristics of rural school districts is complicated by inconsistencies between available data and school district organization.

In contrast, many state school systems are organized so that several school districts exist within one county while other states have county wide school districts which contain both urban and rural schools. Municipal school districts which are independent of surrounding counties are also common among Southern states. In either case, the development of socioeconomic data for areas served by rural schools is difficult, if not impossible, with existing data sources.

In most cases, the number of school districts is larger than the number of counties in the state. The typical Southern state also exhibits wide variation in terms of school and school district size within the state. In short, it is quite likely that education in Southern states is, on the average, more rural in character than it is for the nation as a whole reflecting the higher degree of rurality in the region.

Further, information on school and district size and state enrollments is consistent with Steven's hypothesis of wide variation among rural school districts between and within regions of the nation. At the policy level, choices are required between education and a variety of other programs which compete for tax revenues, and within the school system, administrators and teachers must choose between a variety of options for affecting educational outcomes.

In general, it is recognized that factors outside the school are critical to explaining educational outcomes. Much of the research in the general area of school input-output relationships has focused on relationships between student achievement and educational expenditures. Schools and teachers were found to differ in effectiveness, but differences were not explained by the indicators of quality used in the various studies. Hanushek's results raise serious questions for educational policies formulated on the basis of expenditures of school and teacher characteristics. However, these results do not mean that expenditures are unimportant. As Hanushek notes, "...there seems to be little question that money could count-it just does not consistently do so within the current organization of schools."

Identifying and evaluating effective organizational and program changes appears to be an important priority for those interested in school improvement. A useful approach is the one suggested by Levin. He notes both the interest in school reform and budgetary restraints as reasons for increased attention to the analysis of cost effectiveness. Levin provides a suggested methodology and demonstrates the usefulness of his approach to analyzing educational alternatives.

A key component of such a research effort will involve the establishment of linkages between researchers and education departments in the various states to develop consistent data reporting to support needed research. In addition to evaluating organizational and programmatic changes within the context of schools, there also seems to be a need for additional research on the question of student achievement and relationships to various measures of school inputs.

This is particularly true for efforts which work with more disaggregated data on achievement and a wider range of measures of inputs. For example, work by Summers and Wolfe found that, "many school inputs do matter and that disadvantaged students can be helped by certain types of inputs." They attribute their success in identifying significant relationships to their use of individual student observations and the ability to observe changes in achievement over time. Clearly, more studies with a similar degree of detail could provide useful inputs into policy debates over improving school quality.

More importantly, conclusions regarding the importance of socioeconomic status in explaining educational outcomes have implications for educational improvement programs which are.limited to changing school level inputs. Implications are especially important for the rural South, an area where educational levels and incomes are generally lower than average and where poverty and under unemployment is higher than average.

Following the conclusion about the importance of

socioeconomic status, Hanushek notes that the studies reviewed offered little in the way of insight into exactly how socioeconomic status influences the educational progress of students. As Benson notes, this is a critical question for education policy, and Summers and Wolfe argue that efforts to assist disadvantaged students in schools are dependent on knowing which school inputs are particularly helpful to such students.

They found, for example, that students with lower test scores are distinctly helped by being in classes with higher achieving students, that students from lower income families benefit more from having teachers from higher rated colleges, and that small schools have a larger beneficial effect for black pupils. The former developed a model of home investment in children in which the quality and quantity of bot time and material goods inputs are influenced by the income and education of parents.

Building on this work and that of others, Benson specifically examines relationships between socioeconomic status and the amount of time spent with children and the nature of the child-parent interactions. He found positive relationships between socioeconomic status and time available for children, the degree of cultural activities, and the extent of parent involvement in both school and non-school activities. Finally, in the area of educational input-output relationships, there is ample evidence to support the idea that communities play a role in educational achievement. Clearly, localities are important from the standpoint of providing financial support, and recent work by Smith argues that economic opportunities existing in the community may influence levels of support for education and the quality of school systems. The latter argument is that high quality jobs with higher educational requirements increase student-family expectations regarding returns to education and also increase community expectations of the school system in terms of quality education programs.

The role of the community, however, is even more pervasive in influencing school outcomes. In his household model of human capital formation, Benson allows for what he terms "neighborhood effects" noting that, "It is unrealistic to assume that attitudes and actions are confined within the single family." The idea is that through interactions with other children and families within a neighborhood, students receive either positive or negative reinforcement relative to actions in the school or within their own family.

In other words, the ability of parents and schools to influence student progress is, in some way, dependent on the community. An idea similar to that of Benson has been developed more formally by Coleman. He recognizes the role of physical, financial and human capital, and then he suggests an additional "social capital" found to reside in relationships among people within a community. More importantly, Coleman argues that social capital is important in the creation of human capital. Coleman's work is best illustrated with brief reference to his research.

He notes that students (both Catholic and non-Catholic) in Catholic schools exhibit dramatically lower drop out rates than do similar students in public schools or in other private schools. Coleman found similar results for students from single-parent families in Catholic schools, students traditionally considered to be at a high risk for dropping out of school. He also found that other religious (non-Catholic) schools have performance characteristics similar to those of Catholic schools with respect to drop out rates.

The policy implications of Coleman's work lie in his explanation of the differences in drop out rates between religious and private schools. Rather than being a function of school quality (school provided inputs), he concludes that the differences are due to the community within which the school functions. The religious tie provides the basis for a community of parents, students, and school personnel, and relationships within this community (social capital) reinforce and support school outcomes.

Funding education remains a major, if not the major, expenditure item in the budgets of state and local government, and questions of equity relating to fiscal capacity, educational needs, and local tax effort are paramount in policy debates.

Importantly, most such issues are directly relevant to questions of improving education in the rural South. Essentially, financing education is a state and local government function with some trend in recent years towards an increased role for state governments. Typically, state funds are allocated to school districts using a formula that makes some effort to account for wealth disparities at the local level.

Federal efforts in educational funding did increase substantially as a part of the "War on Poverty" during the late 1960s and early 1970s. However these funds are restricted to the support of compensatory education programs, and federal funds have never amounted to more than ten percent of total expenditures. Southern states tend to differ from national averages in that states generally provide a larger share of school funds.

Southern states, in general, compare favorably in terms of average instructional salaries as a percent of per capita income in the state. Four states (Arkansas, Florida, Oklahoma, and Virginia) are below the national average, one state (Texas) is close to the average, and other Southern states are above average. Among Southern states, only two states (Kentucky and Louisiana) increased educational expenditures at a rate below that of the nation as a whole, Florida increased expenditures at a rate below that of the nation as a whole, Florida increased expenditures at the same rate as the nation, and all other Southern states exceeded the national average rate of increase. Similar results are indicated for real (inflation adjusted) increases in expenditures.

National data, however, masked considerable variation in spending at the state and local level. State data on education expenditures presented by Jansen revealed higher expenditures in nonmetropolitan counties in all southern states with the exceptions of Tennessee and Virginia in 1982, and in these two states, differences were not large.

However, the fact that considerable variation remained across counties, and the fact noted earlier relative to multi-district counties, precludes a similar conclusion for all nonmetropolitan school districts. The education finance literature recognizes that school finance must consider factors other than the equalization of expenditures - that student needs, program delivery costs, and other factors vary dramatically across school districts. A program based funding approach would focus on the numbers and types of students, the types of programs desired, and the cost of program delivery in particular school environments.

School budgets could then be constructed to deliver specific programs to specific schools. A research effort focusing on program costs would be a prerequisite to implementation of this approach with the first step being the development of data reporting systems designed to allow cost assessment. Unlike state aid in most cases, current federal programs are targeted towards students without consideration for the ability of the state or locality to finance needed educational programs.

Education and Economic Development: Remaining

questions for research and policy analyses focus specifically on the set of relationships between education (or human capital formation in general) and economic development in rural areas. Here, the available evidence is mixed, and there is no clear specification of the role of human capital in economic development. On the one hand, it is difficult to imagine a successful regional (or rural) development effort without high levels of human capital development and quality education systems.

On the other hand, it is equally clear that human capital investment at the local or regional level is only one of t a complex set of interrelated factors influencing economic growth. Further, it seems that the acquisition of human capital is, it self, influenced by a similarly complex set of factors. Understanding these relationships may be the most important set of research needs facing those interested in rural education and rural economic development.

At the national level, Teixeira and Swaim point to an emerging imbalance between the demand and supply of educated workers. The demand for skilled workers is increasing as a result of compositional change among industries and content change in existing jobs. At the same time, a national slowing in the rate of increased educational attainment and declines in cognitive achievement combine to reduce the supply of skilled workers.

Rural Education through Poverty Alleviation

In Rural America, some regions and communities are thriving, others are struggling to survive. During the widespread prosperity of the 1990s, many rural areas continued to suffer persistent poverty. In recent decades, global economic forces and technological change have caused many rural communities to lose their historic job base of mining, farming, timber, or low-wage manufacturing.

Many Indian nations have never been able to develop viable economies on reservations. Other rural communities face a different challenge: rapid growth threatens to overwhelm traditional culture, while the benefits of an expanding economy fail to reach low-income residents. Distressed rural regions are diverse racially, ethnically, and culturally as well as economically.

Their populations include Appalachians, African Americans and whites in the Deep South, many Indian nations, Mexican-Americans and other Hispanics in the Southwest. Despite their differences, these communities share rich cultural traditions and strong values of family and community. They also share common economic and social challenges. In all these regions, education levels are low. Many young people drop out of school; others leave home after high school or college for lack of job opportunities.

Community development efforts struggle to combat the sense of powerlessness that comes from absentee ownership of land and resources, a one-industry economy, or high dependence on government programs and transfer payments. And many communities are divided by conflicts between racial or ethnic groups, between rich and poor, or between natives and newcomers. Rural people deserve opportunities to participate in America's prosperity.

And rural communities have few institutions other than community colleges that can simultaneously work to build a viable economy and educate people for a better life. The Rural Community College Initiative (RCCI) offers a model to help community colleges in distressed areas move their people and communities toward prosperity. The RCCI challenges colleges to think broadly about their potential as catalysts for regional development. It does not impose a particular set of programs or strategies to solve regional problems; rather, it fosters a climate of innovation that will spark local solutions.

The RCCI approach helps colleges, in partnership with their communities, develop effective strategies for economic development and educational access-a process that can put their regions and their people on the road toward economic renewal. The RCCI is grounded in five principles:

1. *Rural America matters. Rural communities are the source of our natural resources as well as many of our values. The heart of America must remain healthy if the body is to survive.*

2. *Healthy communities focus on their assets. Rural America is home to rich cultural traditions and diverse natural environments. Successful communities nurture and build on their natural and human assets to promote prosperity. The RCCI encourages development that is compatible with the valued heritage of rural communities.*

3. *Change begins with self-assessment. A willingness to address community problems and work for institutional change is central to RCCI. The change process begins with an honest, data-driven analysis of community strengths and challenges. This analysis helps the community reach agreement on priorities for action and set attainable goals that reflect its vision for the future.*

4. *Effective change requires collaboration and inclusiveness. The divides of geography, race, wealth, and culture are particular threats to fragile rural communities. Across the country, communities that value diversity and practice collaborative, inclusive decision-making are more successful than those with narrowly held political power or deep race*

and class divisions. Successful communities pay attention to building institutional collaboration, eschewing internal competition, broadening leadership, and promoting shared decision-making. To this end, RCCI strengthens partnerships between the college and the community and brings new voices to the table.

5. *Equity and high expectations should undergird education and economic development goals. The most successful communities are committed to guaranteeing all people-rural and urban, rich and poor-access to high-quality education, with support to help them succeed in school and in the economy.*

The RCCI stresses economic development and access to education as concurrent goals because both are needed to revitalize distressed rural areas. Economic development can create jobs, income, and wealth. But economic development often fails to benefit poor people. Even in a growing economy, people with weak education and skills cannot get good jobs. And even in a thriving region, lack of access to capital and business know-how prevents many potential entrepreneurs from starting successful businesses.

Education and training are essential to help individuals gain access to good jobs, wherever they choose to live. But without a strong economy, many rural people have to leave their communities to find work. The link between economic development and access to education is especially important in poor rural regions. In these places, low levels of educational attainment and high poverty are barriers to development that must be addressed directly if the economy is to thrive.

Rural community colleges and tribal colleges are uniquely positioned to be catalysts for increasing economic and educational opportunity in their communities. They are "common ground" institutions, respected by the public, private, and nonprofit sectors. Compared to most institutions, they are trusted by people across social classes. They can convene diverse groups of people to work on community problems; they can help create a collaborative civic culture, part of the foundation for community prosperity. They have the stature, the stability, and the flexibility to provide leadership for regional development.

Community colleges are active on both the supply and demand side of the labor market, working to create jobs while preparing people to fill those jobs. Indeed, they are the only institutions with the capacity for both place-based economic development and people-based education and training strategies. As flexible institutions with a broad mission, community colleges have the potential to build bridges within their communities and regions. For young people, they can bridge the gap between high school and postsecondary education or work.

For adults, they can provide links to basic education, occupational training, a baccalaureate degree, and good jobs. Community colleges can connect employers with qualified workers, cutting-edge technology, and improved forms of workplace organization. And they can link potential entrepreneurs with resources for successful business operation.

Despite their strengths, community colleges cannot achieve RCCI goals on their own. There are many forces-both internal and external to the community-that bear on community vitality and prosperity. In seeking to expand educational and economic opportunity, the college operates in a complex environment that includes the economic system (with many levels, from local to international), the educational system, and multiple tiers of government.

The environment alsoencompasses social values and

norms that shape the behavior of individuals, families, civic organizations, businesses, and government. And it includes other institutions that influence community affairs, such as local newspapers and grassroots organizations. On its own, the college has direct influence in just one of these spheres-education. But even in that sphere, many factors affect the college's ability to expand educational access-the nature of local K-12 schools, public investment in higher education, local job opportunities, cultural values about education, to name just a few.

In the realm of economic development, the college occupies an even less central position. The RCCI experience has shown there is much that colleges can do as catalysts for improved education and economic opportunity, but they cannot do it alone. The multifaceted environment in which the college operates, coupled with the ambitious goals of economic development and educational access, calls for deep college/ community collaboration.

Besides providing an effective way to address community problems, such collaboration can also strengthen the college as an institution. To encourage effective collaboration between college and community, the RCCI process begins with a leadership team representing both the college and the community. In RCCI, "economic development" means creating jobs, raising incomes, generating wealth, and reinvesting that wealth in the region's businesses, institutions, and people.

It means increasing the overall level of economic activity in the region-creating opportunities for people to start and operate profitable businesses, do productive work, and raise their standard of living. And it means targeting economic opportunity to people who have been left out. Each community or region needs to define the kind of development it seeks based on the values of its people, its assets-including natural and human resources, cultural resources, and existing economic strengths-and its constraints or weaknesses. It is not always easy for a community to agree on a vision for developing its economy.

Many communities debate the trade-offs between growth and environmental or cultural preservation. In some rural communities, including Indian reservations, there is deep-rooted ambivalence toward a capitalistic, money-centered economy. Before signing on to an economic development agenda, people want to know how it will lead to a better life. The RCCI encourages each community to define economic development in harmony with local values and set appropriate goals that will lead toward prosperity.

Economic development efforts often focus on job creation by encouraging new business start-ups, helping existing businesses expand, and recruiting businesses to the region. But in many rural communities, the foundation for business development must first be put in place. That foundation includes technology and capital; a well-prepared workforce; a culture of entrepreneurship; sound physical infrastructure; and strong civic and social infrastructure, including broad-based leadership, good schools, competent local government, health care, child care, and strong community organizations.

In the past, much rural economic development relied on exploitation of natural resources or recruitment of industry, often marketing cheap land and labor as community "assets." In an era of global competition, those old approaches will not yield positive, sustainable results. Today, a community's economic prospects depend on a flexible, well-trained workforce, good public schools, access to technology and capital, cultural and natural amenities, and a strong civic infrastructure. Today's successful communities are those that help their existing businesses become more productive and competitive, as well as assisting new business start-ups.

They take a regional approach, working across town and county lines to build on common strengths. And they work to strengthen their foundation for development, especially their civic infrastructure. Increasingly, the notions of "civic capacity" and "social capital" are helping people understand what makes for healthy communities and strong local economies. Civic capacity refers to factors such as the vitality of local leadership and local government, citizen involvement in civic affairs, and the breadth and capabilities of community organizations.

The related notion of social capital encompasses relationships, networks, and bonds of trust among people that facilitate problem-solving and collective action within a community. Based on the experience of MDC and other researchers and practitioners, communities that make the surest progress toward improving quality of life for all citizens are those with a culture of inclusion, engagement, and democracy. These are places where voices from all sectors of the community are heard in solving community problems-including newcomers, women, lower-income people, members of racial and ethnic minority groups, and people with unconventional views.

To bring new voices to the table, communities must have the "will" to become more just, fair, and democratic, and they must be open to new ideas. Successful communities practice open, inclusive decision-making. They work to strengthen leadership and group process skills so more people can participate effectively in broad-based decision-making. Equally important are interpersonal relationships. Successful communities benefit from a critical mass of trusting relationships that cut across lines of race, class, religion, and neighborhood.

These relationships enable leaders of diverse constituencies to work together on common problems. Another characteristic of successful communities is a sense of shared responsibility and consensus around a common vision for the future. When leaders from business, government, education, and community organizations-along with diverse, ordinary citizens-recognize their common interests and reach "alignment," working together toward common goals, the community is more likely to move ahead.

Finally, a healthy local economy depends not only on private entrepreneurs but also "civic entrepreneurship." People scout out promising models for community revitalization, develop innovative responses to local problems, and volunteer their time for community development efforts. Capable organizations initiate projects and services that are not provided by government or business.

Community colleges can make important contributions to building all these underpinnings for economic development-inclusive decision-making, broadcivic engagement, stronger bonds of trust across the community, alignment around a common vision for the future, and a spirit of civic entrepreneurship and innovation. Economic development in Indian Country presents special challenges akin to those in developing countries.

Indian nations are isolated from mainstream America, with poor infrastructure, weak governments, and little access to capital. Poverty is endemic. As with other developing countries, the native nations of America must reassume control over their tribal assets, tribal institutions, and tribal governments before they can build a new economy. This transformation is slowly taking shape in Indian Country under the rubric of "nation-building."

For many decades, life in Indian Country was dominated

by centrally controlled federal government programs. Today, American Indian leaders are on a steep learning curve when it comes to managing tribal assets and accessing and managing capital from nongovernment sources. They must also contend with the volatility of political strife in Indian communities. Nevertheless, they know that education and strong governance are keys to long-term development.

The Harvard Project on American Indian Economic Development maintains that economic development on reservations is first and foremost a political challenge. To build their economy, Indian nations must first develop: (1) stable institutions and policies; (2) fair and effective dispute resolution; (3) separation of politics from business management; (4) a competent bureaucracy; and (5) a form of government that is compatible with tribal culture.

The goal of most local economic development programs is simply "job creation." The RCCI urges rural communities to delve deeper in setting their goals by asking, "What outcomes do we seek?" Objectives might include diversification of the economy, greater local ownership of businesses, higher-skill/ higher-wage jobs, drawing new income to the region, or targeting development efforts to benefit the poorest citizens. Different objectives point to different strategic approaches. If job creation is the central objective, it is important to recognize that not all jobs are created equal. This is true not just in terms of job quality (for instance, wages, benefits, job security, occupational safety) but also in terms of impact on the regional economy.

The most important distinction is between "economic base" businesses that bring new income into the region and service/ retail businesses that recirculate consumer dollars within the region. Retail and service businesses typically serve local customers. These firms are important for rural communities-

they offer convenience (for instance, a grocery store close to home) and they prevent consumer dollars from leaking out of the region. But a regional economy cannot be built on service businesses alone.

Regional economies thrive based on their ability to export products (for instance, through manufacturing) and import dollars (for instance, through tourism). Regions that find ways to build their economic base will have a stronger economy in the long run. Successful economic development efforts identify and build on the region's competitive advantages. These can include strengths such as existing industry clusters, workforce capabilities, natural and cultural resources.

Successful communities also recognize that today's competitive advantage may not be tomorrow's. They improve their long-term prospects by looking entrepreneurially for new opportunities, rather than just protecting their current economic niche. Economic Development Approaches for the Future New economic realities in rural America demand new approaches to economic development.

Rural development experts looking toward the next century urge communities to develop their human resources and a sound civic infrastructure, to assist new and existing businesses, and above all to take a collaborative, regional approach to development. Across the country, workforce education is community colleges' most widely recognized contribution to economic development. Colleges prepare workers for technical occupations, upgrade the literacy skills of adults in the workplace, and in many states, provide customized training for employers.

In addition to workforce preparation, there are several other ways in which community colleges can provide support and leadership for economic development. These are especially important in rural areas, where there are often few institutions other than the community college that can perform these functions. Rural community and tribal colleges have acted as catalysts for economic development in the following ways:

1. Strengthening the foundation for economic development through civic capacity-building. Community colleges can help build civic capacity by convening stakeholders to develop a unified vision for the community and by nurturing a broad-based cadre of community leaders. They can also help strengthen a web of innovative organizations prepared to respond to community challenges.

2. Act as conveners to build a unified vision for the community' s future. A widely held, shared vision for the future can help a community move toward prosperity and equity. A community college can build this alignment by convening leaders from business, government, education, agriculture, and community-based organizations, helping them develop a positive vision for the community and supporting them in working toward common goals.

Rural community change often is impeded by the small size and homogeneous make-up of local leadership. Expanding the leadership base can bring the community new energy, new ideas, and new directions, especially in communities with high poverty, deep race or class divisions, and narrowly held political and economic power. Create new organizations to lead community development work. In most rural communities, the nonprofit sector is small and fragile. Funding for nonprofits is limited and tenuous, and most organizations focus on a narrow area of activity. Yet nonprofits increasingly are recognized as important players in facilitating community change and providing services not offered by the public or private sectors.

In RCCI, college/community teams have provided

leadership to create or strengthen organizations such as community development corporations, community foundations, Indian chambers of commerce, and a special fund to provide water-and-sewer services for low-income rural homes. Initiating and strengthening entrepreneurship and small business development programs. In distressed rural areas with few large employers, growing healthy small businesses is a particularly important economic development strategy.

Many rural colleges operate small business centers that offer counseling, technical assistance, and skills workshops; and RCCI urges them to set high-quality standards for their services. Additional college strategies in support of small business include: developing and managing business incubators (including specialized incubators for e-commerce, food products, or other types of businesses); working with banks and other institutions to create new loan funds or other strategies to make more capital available to rural businesses; providing specialized support to self-employed artisans; offering entrepreneurship courses to help more people start and operate successful businesses; and seeking out or developing entrepreneurship curricula that are in harmony with local culture and values.

3. Promoting a regional approach to economic development. Whenever possible, RCCI encourages communities to work regionally to develop their economy. For too long, rural towns and counties have approached economic development as a competition against their neighbors. In today's highly competitive global economy, small communities achieve more when they pool resources, identify common assets, and work together to develop the regional economy.

Community colleges are natural leaders in this arena because most serve multicounty areas. Strategies tested by RCCI colleges include: leading regional or reservation-wide tourism initiatives; initiating regional planning efforts; and uniting regional leaders to design regional economic development initiatives.

4. Coordinating a regional workforce development system attuned to employers' changing needs. Community colleges enhance their regions' competitiveness when they work closely with employers to design and deliver high-quality education and training at a variety of levels. These include: basic and advanced skills training for existing workers; customized training for expanding firms; workshops to help managers implement quality standards for the high-performance workplace; training in teamwork and related skills to help workers adjust to new workplace demands.

5.Promoting technology transfer and competitiveness. Just as the Extension Service has helped spread new agricultural technology among farmers during the 20th century, 21st century rural America needs an institution to help small and mid-sized businesses adopt new technologies. Community colleges can play important roles by organizing manufacturing networks, serving as brokers between firms and sources of specialized technical assistance, and developing programs tailored to key sectors in the regional economy. These services, along with high-quality workforce training, can have significant impact on the stability and expansion of local businesses.

6. Developing programs that target poor people while creating jobs. Too often, the fruits of the best-intended economic development efforts fail to reach the people who most need jobs and income. Some economic development strategies address this challenge head-on. These include: school-based enterprises (which teach entrepreneurship and business management skills while creating actual businesses based at a high school or community college); microenterprise programs for welfare recipients and other low-income people; youth community service programs (which provide education, job skills, and heightened self-esteem for participants while supporting community development efforts); and targeted job training for new and expanding industries (which gives poor people direct access to new jobs created as a result of successful economic development initiatives).

7. Encouraging a strong education ethic. Throughout the 19th and 20th centuries, most jobs in rural America required little formal education. The rural economy failed to provide an incentive for completing high school, let alone college. Today, the playing field has shifted-education is a prerequisite for both individual and community prosperity-but many people have not heard the message. Community colleges can be a powerful force for economic development by encouraging a strong education ethic in their regions.

Accessing Educational Opportunity

Providing broad access to education is central to the community college movement, and community colleges pride themselves on extending an "open door" to all in their service area. Indeed, rural community colleges serve a broad socioeconomic cross section of the population, and RCCI colleges serve large numbers of the rural poor. There are particular populations, however, that face special barriers to education and employment: they are the people for whom "college" is often an alien idea and a forbidding institution.

If they are to enroll and succeed in college programs and secure good jobs, the college needs to provide not just passive accessibility through open admissions and low tuition but active, aggressive outreach, counseling, support, and job placement. For RCCI, the term "access" encompasses both access to the college and access through the college to expanded opportunities-including further education and productive, rewarding work.

Middle school and high school students-especially those at risk of dropping out of high school and those enrolled in academically weak programs that prepare them neither for college nor for work. Community college students whose weak academic skills or need for support services threatens their success. Adults and out-of-school youth (including high school dropouts and welfare recipients) who are unemployed, marginally employed, or have given up looking for work.

Adults in the workforce who need new skills, including recently dislocated workers and those in danger of losing their jobs due to changes in technology or workplace reorganization. People living in remote areas who seek education but cannot travel the long distance to the college campus.

New economic realities in rural America demand an expanded definition of access. The RCCI encourages colleges to be aggressive about increasing access to education, training, and productive and rewarding work. This means reaching out to disadvantaged populations and offering appropriate programs that take peoplefrom "where they are to where they want to be." RCCI colleges have increased access to education in the following ways:

Building partnerships with secondary schools. Community colleges can play a powerful role in raising academic standards and achievement levels in middle schools and high schools. They can encourage more young people to prepare for and enroll in college, and they can help students make a successful transition to college and career. Proven strategies include: coordinating a high-quality regional Tech Prep program; developing "bridge" programs that offer career education, academic enrichment, mentoring, and dropout prevention for middle and high school students; joint faculty development and curriculum development for the college and secondary schools; dual enrollment courses which enable high school students to earn college credit; and organizing citizens and educators to improve education at all levels from preschool through adult.

Helping all students achieve success. Economically and educationally disadvantaged students face particular barriers to academic success. To serve these students effectively, the college first needs to create a welcoming environment for those who may feel intimidated by the very concept of college. To help students complete programs and advance to further education and jobs, the college needs to provide strong support services such as counseling, tutoring, mentoring, financial aid, child care, and transportation. And it needs to help faculty and staff adopt techniques for working effectively with disadvantaged students.

RCCI colleges have demonstrated several ways to reach disadvantaged populations and increase student success: Reach out aggressively to disadvantaged and minority students. Rural community colleges in high-poverty regions typically enroll many low-income students. Even so, RCCI challenges colleges to assess whether any disadvantaged populations may be underserved.

Sometimes such scrutiny shows relatively low enrollment for minorities or people from certain geographic districts. Strategies include hiring minority recruiters to work in minority high schools and neighborhoods, and establishing outreach centers in underserved communities. Many potential students never enroll in college programs-or enroll and drop out-because of family or community barriers. For instance, women may experience family resistance to their educational or career aspirations; students with family responsibilities may drop out when problems at home eclipse their studies.

Some community colleges are beginning to view students holistically, in the context of family and community. As important as specific strategies are faculty and staff who understand and support their students. An emerging concern at rural community colleges is the declining enrollment of male students. In some economies, men stay away from college because they can find work despite their low education levels. But increasingly in many rural areas, men languish unemployed and unemployable while women prepare themselves for an economic future.

Some colleges are experimenting with ways to draw in more male students, from marketing targeted to men to providing mentoring and support services for male students. Help students move beyond developmental courses into college-level programs. Many students who enter college with low academic skills never advance beyond developmental studies. This can change if the college integrates developmental studies with college-level courses and provides appropriate support for at-risk students.

All students learn better when they feel valued, and for students from racial and ethnic minorities, this includes affirming their cultural heritage. Historically, Native Americans, Appalachians, Latinos, and other rural minority groups have seen their cultures belittled by educational institutions and disrupted by outsiders and newcomers to their regions. Tribal colleges in particular have shown how to integrate traditional culture into the curriculum in a way that makes education more meaningful and builds students' pride in themselves and their community. This in turn helps students succeed academically.

Ensure that community college students can transfer successfully to four-year institutions. In low-income rural areas, a high proportion of students who seek a baccalaureate begin their college education at the community college. To help students transfer successfully to a baccalaureate program, the college must ensure high academic standards in transfer courses, work out articulation agreements with four-year colleges and universities, and counsel students about their options.

Offering nontraditional programs to meet the needs of nontraditional students. With reduced federal support for job training and welfare programs, it is more important than ever for community colleges to reach out to hard-to-serve populations including high school dropouts, welfare mothers, and older, dislocated workers. Many of these adults are not presently candidates for traditional college curricula.

They need job-readiness preparation, improved literacy skills, and referral to other employment-related services. In many rural communities, the college is best positioned to coordinate these services. Job readiness. The community college, in conjunction with other community organizations, needs special staff to reach out to unemployed adults, to counsel them and refer them to programs tailored to their needs. The college may be the best place to provide the instruction they need-including literacy and occupational skills, personal motivation and self-esteem, and job-seeking skills. Once they are employed, the college can link these adults to the continued education and training they need to advance beyond an entry-level job.

In many communities adult literacy programs are fragmented and unrelated to the demands of the workplace. Colleges should work with the local organizations that sponsor adult basic education to insure that programs are accessible, of high quality, and helpful in preparing adults for the workplace. Many rural community colleges offer literacy instruction in workplaces, tailored to the specific needs of workers and employers. Under the federal Workforce Investment Act, the hub of employment and training programs are one-stop centers that connect people to education, training, and employment.

Community colleges are an ideal institution to house these centers since they have relationships with both job seekers and employers, and they can provide both short-term and lifelong education and training. In sparsely populated rural areas, distance education is an especially useful tool for educational access. The community college can be a catalyst in forming distance education networks and helping partners obtain funding for telecommunications equipment. It can use interactive video to provide specialized college prep courses at isolated high schools and a variety of classes and videoconferences at remote community centers and satellite campuses.

Through agreements with universities, rural community colleges can make baccalaureate and graduate level courses more readily available to rural residents. Rural people and communities face several disadvantages in the digital age. Lagging infrastructure in some rural areas makes telecommunications connections expensive and/or slow. Computer ownership and Internet access are low among low-income, low-education, minority, and rural households-the very populations that predominate in distressed rural regions. And people with the know-how to service computers, manage networks, develop software, and design web pages are scarce in rural communities.

Community colleges-along with K-12 schools and public libraries-can help expand computer and Internet access for low-income people and enhance computer skills in their communities. College-based strategies include: initiating community technology centers where adults and youth can learn to use computers; providing computers and Internet access for faculty and students; organizing low-cost Internet service for the community at large; providing Internet access to businesses through college-run small business assistance centers or business incubators; and developing new curricula to teach computer-related skills.

To be effective catalysts for regional development, community colleges need to do more than launch programs promoting economic development and access to education. They also need to look inward, honing their own ability to anticipate and respond to the needs of the people and communities they serve. They need to build partnerships with other organizations. And the college itself needs an institutional culture that supports innovation, risk-taking, and learning.

The RCCI urges rural colleges to ask themselves how they measure up against the following ideal and to work toward strengthening these essential capacities. A clear institutional mission that encompasses economic development and broad access to education. More than simply having the right words in its mission statement, the college has a deep institutional commitment to the goals of economic development and access. That commitment begins with the president, emanates throughout the administration and faculty, and is shared by the board.

College policies support these dual goals, for instance, by providing incentives for faculty and staff to engage in community service projects. Service to the community is fully integrated into the mainstream of college activity and is valued as highly as more traditional academic functions. The college works collaboratively with elementary and secondary schools, economic development organizations, employers, local governments, and community organizations.

Community members advise the college on its programs and vice versa; there are many collaborative initiatives involving the college and other institutions. College staff have strong knowledge and skills in their fields, and they have the ability to provide leadership for change. Faculty are excellent teachers and use a learner-centered approach in the classroom. Vocational/technical faculty have experience working in their fields and credibility with industry. Appropriate staff are knowledgeable about the regional economy and have frequent interaction with employers.

Staff development provides ample opportunity for continued learning, and there is frequent interaction and collaboration among college departments. College programs are highly regarded by students, employers, and the community at large. Students master what they need to know to be successful in the workplace and in four-year college or university. The college monitors and evaluates its programs and strives for continuous improvement.

Through its planning capacity, the college identifies and responds to trends in the regional and national economies. The college is able to shift its priorities and roles as regional needs change and new opportunities arise. For instance, it develops new curricula to meet the changing needs of individuals and employers. The college's programs and services are well known and valued throughout the region. Also, the college has the ability to raise the funds it needs from government, foundations, individuals, and corporate sources.

In addition to the above capacities, successful rural colleges have certain characteristics that can be considered part of their institutional culture. These characteristics include:

a. *Support for innovation and risk-taking. To develop and sustain the capacities described above, the college needs leadership that is open to new ideas and willing to overcome institutional inertia.*

b. *Becoming a "learning organization." Successful colleges encourage faculty and staff to ask questions and to learn from each other and from the community. They are continually on the lookout for effective practices from around the country and the world that can be adapted to fit the local situation. They seek the counsel of national experts and wise community members. They set aside time for reflection and planning. They look critically at themselves and ask, "How can we improve?"*

c. *Emphasis on equity and excellence. The college sets high standards and provides the support needed to help all students succeed. It has not only an "open door" but a system for bringing the disadvantaged through that door and supporting them along a path to stable careers. The college encourages other educational institutions and employers to do the same.*

d. *Rootedness in local culture. Rural America is rich in cultural traditions. Preservation and celebration of traditional arts, languages, and other cultural practices are increasingly important goals guiding development efforts in many regions, and the community college is an ideal institution to lead these efforts. Integrating local culture into the curriculum also helps students succeed in college by affirming their cultural identity. A faculty and staff that reflects the racial and ethnic makeup of the local population helps make the college a welcoming, supportive place for all students.*

There are many examples of rural colleges-RCCI grantees and others-that perform several of the educational and economic development roles laid out in this paper. Some colleges operate one-stop employment and training centers; others offer assistance to small businesses. Some reach out aggressively to middle and high school students; others provide outstanding services to low literacy adults.

For every college, however, RCCI poses a challenging vision-that of working in partnership with other community institutions to further economic progress and expand educational access. To help achieve that vision, RCCI offers colleges a process that can strengthen collaboration with the range of institutions required to advance economic and educational opportunity. Besides benefiting the region, this collaborative process can also strengthen the college's own institutional capacity and help expand its role in economic development and educational access.

The RCCI process is based on a model for community and institutional change that has proven effective in a variety of settings. It relies on leadership by a college/community team. It includes an intensive planning and implementation process that is grounded in the principles expressed in this conceptual framework document. By its very nature, RCCI demands collaboration. No one individual or agency can bring about the transformation of a rural economy, nor can one institution alone provide full access to education.

Regional development is best achieved through joint efforts of the public and private sectors and cooperation among neighboring towns and counties. This calls for involvement of business leaders, local government officials, public school administrators, economic developers, and other public and private sector leaders representing multiple towns and/or counties. To ensure that economic development and access strategies are targeted effectively to poor people, another set of organizations needs to participate in RCCI planning and implementation.

These include grassroots organizations, human service agencies, churches, and other community groups that represent or work closely with populations in need. As a way of stimulating collaboration among all the above organizations and interests, the RCCI process relies on a broad-based, college/community team to lead planning and implementation efforts. Colleges, like traditional corporations, are accustomed to a hierarchical leadership structure and often find team-led efforts challenging to institute. However, RCCI colleges that have used teams have found the payoff is high. The benefits go beyond just planning and implementation of RCCI-related activities.

In a sense, the process becomes a product in its own right. Strong college/community teams have helped RCCI colleges become more responsive to community needs and strengthened the colleges' place in the community. And by nurturing relationships among community leaders who had not worked together closely in the past, RCCI teams help build the foundation for a stronger community.

A Key to Rural Learning System

The need for knowledge and improved skills to increase food production in developing countries is clear and present. Recent FAO statistics note that more than 65 low-income countries suffer from inadequate food security, with about 790 million people living in hunger.

Another 34 million undernourished people have been identified from countries in transition, mainly in Eastern Europe and the area of the former USSR. All told, as the twentieth century ended, about one in seven people were going hungry. And the prospects for erasing hunger during the first quarter of the third millennium appear daunting.

From a current base of slightly over 6.2 billion people, using the high fertility path, the world's population may exceed eight billion by 2025 and food needs in developing countries - which will account for 98 percent of the population increase - will double.

The 1996 World Food Summit set a target of reducing by half the number of hungry people in the developing world - about 400 million people - by the year 2015. The progress achieved during much of the 1990s, however, has tended to cast this goal as being too optimistic. In the 1990/92 period for example, out of a group of 96 developing countries, the number of undernourished was estimated at 830 million people; by 1995/97 this had dropped to 790 million or a decrease of 40 million overall, a seemingly positive result. A closer look at the data revealed that only 37 countries out of the original 96 had actually reduced the number of undernourished - by about 100 million people combined overall.

Across the rest of almost two-thirds of the developing world, the aggregate number of undernourished actually increased by 60 million. The resulting total net reduction of eight million per year hence reached only 40 percent of the proportional rate of 20 million per year needed to reach the objective. The problem is particularly acute in sub-Saharan Africa.

These sobering results dramatically suggest that unless more effective solutions are found for increasing food production, and better distribution of it, the 2002 World Food Summit's repeat goal of halving the number of hungry people by 2015 - with a concomitant rate of 22 million per year needed to do so - may again fall short. Continuing at the current level would take more than 60 years to reach the Summit's target.

Improved communication to strengthen rural learning is one of the immediate methods in which the problem of food security may be addressed. Indeed, over the past thirty years, research findings have consistently demonstrated that audience-oriented communication strategies can play a catalytic role in accelerating the rate of agricultural technology transfer through providing relevant information, changing negative attitudes, and skills training.

Initially, "small media" were mainly used (e.g. video, radio, flip-charts, illustrated pamphlets, village theatre) with content tailored to a given community, province or region. Communication approaches ranged from multimedia campaigns to support for group meetings conducted by extension agents, and materials to strengthen interpersonal communication.

Over time, participatory methods were refined to bring in the views of the intended beneficiaries from the start in designing project goals and selecting appropriate communication and adult learning methods to support implementation. At the turn of the twentyfirst century, as wireless infrastructures span the globe, a growing number of development specialists and agencies argue that appropriate use of information and communication technologies (ICTs) offer alternative solutions to erasing chronic food deficits.

Using the Internet to seek out research-based recommendations, combining them with indigenous practices, and then rendering messages for farmers into locally-friendly formats such as vernacular radio, are currently seen as blending the best of older media and emerging technologies. The challenge in assisting farmers to produce more food implies the need for new technologies, new skills, changed attitudes and practices, and new ways to collaborate.

All of this requires that farmers have access to what they consider to be relevant information and knowledge. Participatory communication and education have thus become what many consider to be the key links between farmers, extension, and research, for planning and implementing consensus-based development initiatives. Too often, however, they have been missing links and many projects have failed as a result.

To redress this oversight, the World Bank and FAO have jointly proposed a framework for reforming agricultural knowledge and information systems for rural development (AKIS/RD) wherein farmers are considered to be at the heart of the "knowledge triangle". Communication and education, research, and extension consequently become services designed to respond to farmers' needs for knowledge to improve their productivity, incomes, welfare and sustainable natural resource management.

Communication-based Adult Rural Learning System

In carrying out its field work, much of FAO's early activities in applying communication for development and rural learning were subsumed within two main areas:

1) *information dissemination and motivation, and*

2) *education and training for field workers and rural producers.*

In practice, the activities are often considered to be interchangeable, as part of a common rural learning strategy. Information dissemination and motivation as the most basic areas of communication were concerned with simply informing rural people of new ideas, services and technologies, and changing attitudes toward improving their quality of life.

The outcomes of education and training, however, rested more in the acquisition and development of new or advanced skills, whether intellectual such as the comprehension of concepts and processes, or physical such as the mastery of tools and practices. The movement toward participatory audience involvement, which was recommended as standard practice during the 1990s, is currently assumed to be a prerequisite in designing each area.

Most of adult learning in rural settings falls under the rubric of non-formal education which can be defined as any organized, systematic educational activity carried on outside the framework of the formal system to provide selected types of learning to particular subgroups in the population.

Formal systems are highly organized and based upon selective entry dependent upon prior success, with content built around a fixed curricula, and with termination or graduation based upon external standards set by a teacher, organization or governmental certifying body.

Non-formal education, in contrast, is flexible, open to anyone, with content dedicated to concrete issues for application in day-to-day life - in short, a continuous learning process highly relevant to the immediate environment. At its best, it is founded on a participatory and interactive approach with farmers becoming partners and key actors in their own development projects.

The emphasis is placed on sharing of knowledge between technical experts and rural people. The process begins by "listening to rural people" and a shift to farmer-led identification of learning and training needs through critical reflection based on practical experience. Knowledge sharing among researchers, communicators, extensionists, educators, and farmers thus recognises the importance of indigenous knowledge bases as a priori conditions to examining how new research recommendations might best fit into them, and before grafting on new technologies.

Along with the levelling of extension services to match farmer demands, a shift from teaching them to learning with them - through practical applications - has assumed vital importance. Labelled as a "constructivist" approach to education, continuous learning is always a unique product "constructed" as each individual combines new information with existing knowledge and experiences.

And because learning from a constructivist view is so entwined with one's experiences, the primary role of the extension worker in farmers' learning processes thus becomes one of facilitating problem definition and prioritizing technology solutions as prerequisites to designing training packages for presentation back to them.

This has prompted a rethinking of the design of formal learning systems for extension workers, particularly at the post-secondary level. To ensure relevance to field operations within academic programmes, participatory curriculum development is being advocated among the key stakeholders themselves, the farmers. The farmers' role in the development of education and training courses is especially important because farmers can voice their needs based upon practical experience and gain a direct benefit from the outputs.

Communication approaches for rural learning currently range from interpersonal exchanges, group processes (including farmer field schools), mass media (principally radio), mixed-media campaigns, conventional media combined with Internet delivery available from community telecentres, and distance education.

Interpersonal Communication

Interpersonal communication is fundamental to learning and change in rural areas and no amount of media can supplant it when it comes to adding persuasiveness and credibility to messages. Whether it be in the form of a skilled extension worker making his/her rounds, or farmers learning from other farmers, when it comes down to making a decision with regard to a new technology or changing farming practices, interpersonal sources often make the difference between adoption or rejection.

Methods to improve farmer to farmer and extension agent communication include simple, mostly visually illustrated pamphlets, and leaflets. Spontaneous drama, poems and songs based on farmers' own experiences have also proved effective.

Training for extension workers has been mainly directed toward perfecting their interpersonal communications skills, and, more recently, in facilitating participatory involvement of farmers in defining their own problems, reaching consensus on actions to be taken, information and skills development required to carry out the actions, and mechanisms for seeking research assistance on technical problems for which there is no ready solution available locally.

In this cycle extension workers have the responsibility of helping farmers to articulate their problems to research agencies and then assisting them to adapt and apply the results. Training for rural producers, typically involving extension or subject matter specialists as vital interpersonal links, has tended to rely on group media such as slides, film-strips, audio-cassettes, flip-charts, village theatre, and video.

In the hands of a trained facilitator these media add punch and authority to a presentation. Perhaps the most advantageous aspect of group media is the possibility for immediate feedback from the audience and establishment of a two-way flow of information. Participants' level of understanding can be tested, central points can be repeated where necessary, and discussions can be started with a view toward initiating action on agreed upon development problems.

Cases abound where FAO has produced film-strips and slides with audio commentaries for extension meetings. Normally the presentations are reinforced by booklets which depict the visuals used in the script with accompanying dialogue. Routinely, the booklets become manuals in their own right. The prerecorded audio-cassette is another low-cost medium, which FAO has promoted extensively.

The cassette's chief advantage over radio is the control that a group facilitator has over the information flow and the ability to start and stop at will, and repeat messages. In addition, cassette recordings are a convenient way to bring farmers' questions and information needs to the attention of extension and research.

Folk media in the form of popular singers and musicians have also proven highly effective for focusing community attention on a range of topics, including population education and HIV/AIDS mitigation and prevention. Flip-charts have proved particularly useful as extension discussion tools.

Although research at the field level is scarce, a 1998 FAO study in Namibia showed that the use of two flip-charts to explain the benefits of using certified millet seeds along with recommended agricultural practices was positive. When compared to framers who had not been exposed to the visual materials and extension agent explanations, farmers who were part of the extension communication programme increased their planting of certified seeds by 24 percent, and seeding in rows and use of fertilizers each by 23 percent.

Equally impressive, almost half of the participating farmers agreed that the use of flip-charts by extensionists "helped them greatly to understand the improved farming practices". Of all the group media, however, video has emerged as the lead medium of choice for supporting participatory farmer training in a variety of FAO rural development projects. Its many advantages are unequalled by any other medium, namely, its production "immediacy" with instant replay in the field to check on shooting details, its ability to add commentary in local languages, its ease of editing, and its "show anywhere, anytime" flexibility using battery or generator operated playback equipment where electricity is lacking.

During extensive long-term projects in Peru, Mexico, and Mali, FAO has perfected a complete learning package - often referred to as a model for international reference - which combines video with discussion, simple printed materials, and practical work. A more recent example reported by FAO involved a CIDA funded project for training women farmers in Jamaica wherein video was supported with drama performances, oral testimonies and printed materials.

An application of group learning using a variety of media along with direct field experience, one which has proven effective and is growing in popularity, is the Farmer Field School or FFS pioneered by FAO in the Indonesia National Integrated Pest Management (IPM) Programme in 1989. IPM has since evolved into Integrated Production and Pest Management (IPPM).

The guiding principal for a given FFS is that farmers meet on a regular basis to carry out practical learning exercises that combine indigenous knowledge with scientific recommendations. Courses take place in the field, field conditions define the curriculum, and real field problems are observed from planting of a crop through to harvesting. An FFS is usually initiated by someone who has had experience in growing the crop concerned.

For this reason, most IPPM initiatives have begun with training extension field staff in basic technical skills for managing all aspects of crop production. Each school lasts for one cropping season, with a group of about 25 people meeting on a weekly basis to study and make decisions based on the cropping calendar (e.g. seeding, fertilizing, weeding, curbing pest encroachment). Instead of listening to lectures or watching demonstrations, farmers observe, record and discuss what is happening in the field.

This hands-on, discovery-learning approach generates a deep understanding of ecological concepts and their practical application. In the process, farmers are transformed from recipients of information to generators and manipulators of field-validated local data. FFSs are always held in the community where the farmers live, with the extension officer travelling to the site on the day when the school meets.

The field used for study is usually small, and either provided by the community or some other arrangement so that farmers can carry out risk-free management decisions that they might not otherwise attempt on their own farms. All FFSs include field-based pre- and post-tests for the participants. Those with high attendance rates and who master the tests are awarded a certificate. Graduates from an FFS may also take over the job of extension facilitator by doing farmer-to farmer training or most of the functions in a follow-up season's training.

Empirical studies of IPPM-FFS compared with conventional practices show that IPPM methods increase both production and profits. Since 1990 FAO estimates that more than two million farmers have graduated from FSSs in more than 40 countries drawn from Asia, Africa and the Americas.

Given that one-third of adults in the developing world are illiterate, and particularly those in Africa (44 percent), the broadcast media and principally radio have performed a major service in information dissemination. Not surprisingly, with the advent of the transistor receiver, and lowering of prices, radio, either battery operated or wound-up by hand, became the ubiquitous medium for rural communication, a status that it is likely to retain well into the twentyfirst century.

Much of the early emphasis in the 1970s, however, was on open broadcasting for unorganized audiences within a national or regional reach, and typically carried out in isolation from direct involvement of farmers or extension in its programming. In the face of the criticism that by "attempting to reach everyone, it reached no one", open broadcasting for educational purposes, including agricultural programming, was given low priority, averaging less than five percent of total broadcasting hours.

As a stand-alone medium, however, its main value was in reaching a lot of people quickly with fairly simple messages. Attempts to improve the educational value of open broadcasting as a "magic multiplier" to enhance extension included the creation of radio farm forums directed to organised farming groups, built around the format "listen, discuss, act".

A seasoned leader introduced each broadcast topic, initiated follow-up discussion after the broadcast, and coordinated action on its recommendations. The idea was originally developed in Canada during the 1940s and subsequently adapted in a number of developing countries including Ghana, Zambia, Guatemala, Thailand and Senegal. A common problem experienced in most was the difficulty in maintaining active group attendance over an extended period of time since the farm forum was initiated when radio sets were expensive and access was limited.

With the advent of cheap transistor sets individual ownership became more common, lessening the appeal of regular attendance using a shared village radio. A trend toward a mix of private and public sector broadcasting, as a result of deregulation in many countries, also provided competition through a broader range of channels and topics for rural audiences. Radio farm forums mostly disappeared during 1980s, and were replaced by listening groups for specific themes (e.g. rural women's communication needs).

Typically, these include groups of about 15 people who meet to listen to and discuss a weekly half-hour radio broadcast, under the direction of a trained group leader who is supplied in advance with programme guide manuals. An accompanying textbook with each chapter covering a specific radio programme is provided to each participant as a reinforcer.

Other materials might include posters, T-Shirts and dresses bearing topic-related logos. With the current surge of community radio on the one hand and decentralization of capital city-based networks to include regional and local stations on the other, a radio rejuvenation appears to be under way, one that depends upon active audience participation during production and for feedback.

Based on the outcomes of a regional workshop in Africa during 1996, FAO remains firm in its conviction that "Radio remains the most popular, accessible, and cost-effective means of communication for rural people. Radio can overcome the barriers of distance, illiteracy and language diversity better than any other medium".

Radio, whether national, regional or localized-community in reach has also formed the main stay for many multimedia campaigns, the most powerful of strategies in disseminating information and building motivation. Communication theory has tended to support the case for multimedia use based on the premise that having access to at least two channels allows a production team to present and reinforce the same points in different ways and with varied emphasis.

Individuals also differ in their processing of information from different media; some learn better from and prefer visual media than audio and vice versa. In general, evidence from controlled classroom studies suggests that providing a variety of reinforcing channels caters to both learning styles and learning preferences. More practical findings from the field, however, especially in rural development, are rare but convincing where systematically documented.

The importance of popular participation in planning and executing rural projects was first postulated during the 1970s when it was suggested that the "dominant paradigm" of top-down planning would shift toward self-development wherein villagers and urban poor would be the priority audiences, and self-reliance and building on local resources would be emphasized.

The role of communication in this process would be 1) providing technical information about development problems and possibilities, and about appropriate innovations in answer to local requests, and 2) circulating information about the self-development accomplishments of local groups so that other such groups might profit from others' experience. Despite these early predictions, rural communication systems continued to service the transfer of technology or "TOT" model in which information passed from researchers to farmers though the extension system.

At least a decade would pass before participatory methodologies began to gain acceptance. And where they were tentatively introduced, most projects up to end of the 1980s were mainly concerned with having beneficiaries discuss how to implement projects or "functional participation". The practice of full "interactive participation", a product of the 1990s, started with beneficiaries deciding which development initiatives should be pursued, whether the initiatives were feasible and prioritising those that were, and only then deciding how to carry them out, all the while keeping in mind the requirements for sustainability and possibly "self-mobilization" upon project completion.

One of FAO's first exercises in "interactive participation" in communication and learning for community development was carried out over a three-year period in the Philippines from 1991-1994. Building on the mounting literature in participatory rural appraisal (PRA), and refinement of its methodology, the overriding goal of the project was to take each of five pilot-communities or barangays through prototype exercises in setting priorities for technology transfer.

This involved bottom-up needs assessment through a number of PRA tools (social and livelihood mapping, seasonal calendar, problem trees, key informant panels, media access and preferences) and quantitative baseline KAP surveys, which served as diagnostic profiles for the framing of communication and learning objectives. A variety of multichannel communication approaches were then implemented, spearheaded by a new lead-medium in the form of community audio-tower systems or CATS, in each participating barangay.

Each CATS consisted of a karaoke system, two microphones, and a 500-watt amplifier housed in a studio and connected to four 100-watt loudspeakers attached to a metal tower. Total cost of each complete unit was about US$2000 provided that construction of studio housing and towers were undertaken through local voluntary participation. "Broadcasting associations" were subsequently formed by each community to manage, produce, and broadcast programmes created by thematic subcommittees, e.g. agriculture, health, cooperatives, and youth, on a weekly schedule.

Networking Telecentres

While the call for "networking" has become highly popularised, sub-Saharan Africa in particular has faced deepening marginalisation. According to data provided by IDRC, in 1999, excluding South Africa, the so-called "digital divide" was reflected in only one African in 9 000 having access to the Internet, while around the world the average was one person in 40.

IDRC has responded with project "Acacia", designed to encourage access to ICTs by low-income groups in cities and the countryside, to provide tools and techniques that make it easier for low-income groups to use ICTs, and to adapt applications and services to meet community needs. The vehicle for doing this is through the establishment of community multimedia centres or telecentres accessible within an hour of home by foot.

Most of its emphasis has thus far been on urban telecentres - which have been mushrooming - with typical services offered consisting of telephone, fax, photocopying, e-mail, Internet, and small group training in ICT proficiencies (e.g. information data navigation, networking, designing Web pages). Pilot telecentres are also being tried out in a limited number of rural settings (e.g. Mali, Uganda, Mozambique and South Africa).

FAO/SDRE has been actively supporting the use of ICTs for agricultural development through rural telecentres, and other means (such as cooperatives and farmer associations), although the pace has been much slower than the explosion in urban settings. Rural community telecentres (RCTs) have much or all of the capability of their urban counterparts as well as access to more traditional media such as audio and video playback equipment.

Typically, they can also serve as venues for formal and non-formal distance education training for extension and subject matter specialists. As information "depots" or "hubs" they can place regional, national and international information at the fingertips of agricultural development workers - information on markets, weather, crops, livestock production and natural resource protection.

Much of the debate revolving around RCTs has been in establishing the link from the global networks to national, town, and finally to village levels, the latter referred to by some as "the last mile" of connectivity and others as "the first mile". Costs appear to be the main constraint. IDRC estimates that if a wired land-based network is to be put into place, the expense for connecting rural subscribers in Africa will be five to ten times higher than that of city dwellers. The cost of equipment, and training of those to operate it, must also be factored in.

But the issues of connectivity, start-up costs and sustainability can be solved, according to the World Bank, through establishing rural telecentres as a "Community Utility", accessible on a pay-to-use basis. Based on IDRC's experience, however, the report card on making RCTs financially viable is still in the making. FAO, more optimistically, suggests that the trend is clearly wireless, mobile, multimedia and broadband ICTs, with costs dropping appreciable.

Undoubtedly, a strong case can be made for using participatory methods to bring crystallised farmer group's technology information needs to telecentres, tapping the relevant data bases available through the Internet that provide useable recommendations, and then packaging the results to respond to local demands and disseminating it through a variety of conventional media, and especially community radio, for maximum reach. Sustainability, in turn, will increase in direct proportion to client's satisfaction of the service.

The Internet has to be clearly and immediately useful or people won't have the motivation to use it. Clearly, the lessons learned through past communication experiences should be applied to current investments in rural telecentres. Approaches that harness the power of ICTs with unique local needs will undoubtedly significantly strengthen the contributions that telecentres can make to rural development.

FAOs initial experience with using the Internet for rural development started in Latin America in the early 1990s when farmer-operated information networks were established in Chile and Mexico. Operating under the banner of FarmNet (the term that has been applied to initiatives growing out of the Latin American experience), linkages were established with agricultural producers, farmer associations, extension services and NGOs using conventional media, such as rural radio, and appropriate use of the new ICTs.

The networks provide data on crops, inputs, markets, weather forecasts, and credit facilities, among other essential topics. All told, it has proven an efficient and cost-effective way for farmers to access local, regional, national and even global sources. For example, transmitting price and market information through computer-based networks has .proven to be 40 percent more economical than using traditional extension methods.

And by knowing market price information in larger centres, it has also increased farmers' profitability in setting local crop selling rates, and a base for better planning of quantities to plant in the future. In one case, by using market information provided through the network, a farmer association was able to sell cotton for US$82 per quintal as opposed to US$72, the price local buyers were trying to impose.

FarmNet is being piloted in Uganda to facilitate information dissemination among national, district and local levels of the Uganda National farmers association. A more recent FAO development, as part of its World Agriculture

Information Centre (WAICENT) initiatives, has been the Virtual Extension, Research and Communication network or VERCON, designed as an open network to improve communication between research and extension and, for those with access, farmers themselves.

Prototype software is being developed which can be readily adapted locally to improve the flow of information between extension and research departments. And by linking a FarmNet to a VERCON, farmers can have better access to technical expertise. At the same time, researchers and extension workers can gain a better understanding of the local, site-specific problems that farmers face and the practices that they apply in their farming systems. A pilot project is currently under way in Egypt to test and refine the VERCON system.

Distance Education in Rural Areas

While distance education (DE) has been recognized as the most significant educational innovation of the latter half of the twentieth century, its application has been mainly in the formal areas of instructional delivery. Initially building on correspondence for home-based study largely using self-instructional print materials, sophisticated institutions such as the Open University in Britain now use a variety of mixed-media support, along with tutorial counselling and library materials available at study centres geographically accessible to virtually all students.

Increasingly, the Internet is being harnessed to delivery complete on-line courses as well as to provide rapid learner feedback and counselling. Within rural development projects, the potential exists for literally thousands of extension agents in Africa, Asia and the Americas to upgrade their credentials from one or two-year post secondary Certificates or Diplomas to B.Sc. first degrees, and even beyond to Masters level qualifications through in-service distance education.

And by using participatory curriculum development methods, these programmes could be tailored to specific needs of extension workers based on their years of practical field experience. The same potential holds for providing pre-service qualification at all levels at a distance. Emerging examples where DE is being applied to extension training include the Open University of Bangladesh which has a B.Sc. Programme in Agriculture and Rural Development targeted at extension agents; Sir Arthur Lewis College in St. Lucia is also developing a post-secondary Certificate programme in Agriculture at a distance for Caribbean extensionists.

Most distance applications in agricultural education and training thus far, however, have been at the non-formal level, mainly using radio and text materials for both individual and group learning at the farmer level, what FAO has recently coined as "distance extension". Short courses at a distance for professional upgrading of extension agents have also been mounted.

Other examples of distance learning for non-formal education include the G.P. Pant University of Agriculture and Technology in Uttar Pradesh, India, which has offered print-based correspondence courses to farmers and rural youth since 1973. About 500 learners are enrolled each year; individual students can select four courses from a list of seventeen options (mostly on cultivation of particular crops, dairy production, and insecticide and fertiliser uses).

A network of 20 District Extension Centres are available for individual counselling and study support. Non-credit certificates are issued to students passing end-of-term examinations in each course. And the Allama Iqbal Open

University of Pakistan (AIOU), established in 1975 as the first open university in the Region, has been offering correspondence courses in income generation activities for rural women since 1986.

Practical course topics range from Poultry farming and Garment Making, to Selling of Home Made Products. Tutorial support is provided through local study centres. The popularity of the Programme is reflected in an enrolment, as of 1996, of about 4 000 learners per semester.

The school of the air (SoA) is another popular variation of using radio for non-formal distance education. Used extensively in the Philippines and Latin America, the technique lends itself to both mass broadcasting and to participatory community radio for individual as well as group learning. Courses cover a variety of areas including literacy, numeracy, and basic education (usually up to primary qualifications).

In the Philippines, seasonal courses spanning a cropping period of four months are offered to farmers on topics such as organic farming methods. Typically broadcast out of local municipal radio stations, a "community-focused" approach is stressed wherein a local farmer, and subject matter specialist work with radio broadcasters in scripting and production. In general, 30-minute programmes are aired five days a week over a four-month season. Print materials serve as complementary resource materials.

SoAs have proven both efficient and effective. In the municipality of "Infanta" in Quezon province in the Philippines, for example, a programme is presently under-way to transform 3 000 hectares of chemically-treated farms to chemical free farms. More than 5 000 farmers will have been trained in two years through a combination of SoA broadcasts and farmer field schools over five seasons using four teams of two extension workers as field facilitators in each.

3

Education and Multigrade Classroom

The multigrade classroom poses a paradox. For children to learn effectively in multigrade environments, teachers need to be well trained, well resourced, and hold positive attitudes to multigrade teaching. However, many teachers in multigrade environments are either untrained or trained in single-grade pedagogy; have few, if any, teaching/learning resources; and regard the multigrade classroom as a poor relation to the better-resourced single-grade classrooms found in large, urban schools and staffed by trained teachers.

It is clear that a strong need exists for training in how to work effectively in multigrade schools to improve learning. We have accumulated a foundation of experiences and knowledge that reflects five goals:

- *Develop an understanding of effective multigrade classroom organization and instructional practices, and draw out implications for use in local settings*
- *Understand effective instructional concepts and practices in literacy development in the multigrade classroom, and draw out implications for use in local settings*

— *Learn how the school and community can serve as valuable resources to each other*

— *Learn how multigrade schools are supervised and managed, and draw out implications for use in local settings*

— *Develop an understanding about how school change affects the ability of teachers to try out new ideas and draw out implications in local settings*

To achieve these goals, the following guidelines have been established to serve as the underlying principles upon which training activities have been planned and carried out. It needs to be kept in mind that such training, depending on the scope, is time intensive, requiring opportunities for research, discussion, observation, and planning.

Learning is best achieved when it addresses the social and cultural context of the learner. Opportunities are provided to describe the educational setting where the knowledge and experiences gained from the training will be applied. Various levels of education are considered:

— *Students and community*

— *Teachers and the classroom*

— *Management and administration, and*

— *Policy decisionmakers.*

The current design of the training incorporates tasks that are responsive to the unique knowledge participants bring to it. Learning is best achieved in a situation that reflects the diverse and complex nature of the situation where it is to be applied. Every effort is made to provide learning experiences that reflect the type of instructional practices found to be effective in multigrade settings. However, since these practices grow mainly from research in western countries, time for reflection and planning for application in geographically and culturally different contexts is built into the training.

Learning is rooted in language. It is through language that we construct knowledge, coming to new understandings. Language and learning are inextricably linked, for individuals and for groups. Therefore, oral and written language is used extensively to explore information about teaching and learning in mixed-age settings.

For learning and knowledge to be beneficial, it must be applied. We believe knowledge is most valuable when it can be put to meaningful use. Therefore, opportunities are provided for developing action plans for use in one's respective educational setting.

The primary purpose is to convey information and promote opportunities for exploring the concepts and practices of multigrade instruction and organization. Opportunities to observe instruction in multigrade schools and to talk with students, teachers, and administrators are important in learning about the various levels of school organization and management.

For parents, the critical issue is whether the multigrade classroom will provide the kind of positive, satisfying, and productive social and learning experience they want for their child in school. For teachers and school leaders, there are multiple issues: whether enrolment distributions necessitate multigrade classes; the nature of parental, teacher, and school leader attitudes to multigrade classes; how best to organize and teach such classes in order to maximize student learning progress and social development.

For researchers, the major focus for many years has been the question of whether student achievement differs in multigrade and single-grade classes. The multigrade class structure is known by various names in different countries;

these include "composite" or "combination" classes, "double" classes, "split" classes, "mixed-age" classes and "vertically grouped" classes.

It is defined as a class in which students of two or more adjacent grade levels are taught in one classroom by one teacher for most, if not all, of the day. Such multigrade classes are embedded within the traditional graded system: students retain their grade-level labels and are promoted through the school with their grade-level cohort.

The latter two structures have an individualized, developmental focus and manifest in a continuous progress rather than lock-step, graded curriculum for class groups of students varying in age. Student groups remain with the same teacher for two or more years. Multigrade and multiage grouping have been clearly distinguished in order to avoid an "apples and oranges" problem at the level of the independent variable.

Teachers are therefore faced with delivering two different curricula to students of twice the age range in the same amount of time-factors, which make these two structures radically different. In 1970, as the multigrade programs became more complex, they began to incorporate individualized instruction, and to become more like open schools. Thus, the achievement effects began to be much smaller.

An appropriate primary program for all children recognizes that children grow and develop as a "whole," not one dimension at a time or at the same rate in each dimension. Thus, instructional practices should address social, emotional, physical, aesthetic, as well as cognitive needs. The primary program flows naturally from preschool programs and exhibits developmentally appropriate educational practices.

In 1988, United Nations Educational, Scientific and Cultural Organization (UNESCO) held a conference with representatives from India, Korea, Maldives, Nepal, Thailand, Philippines, Sri Lanka, and Indonesia. The conference focused on innovative approaches to teaching disadvantaged groups and teaching in the multigrade classroom. The problems and learning difficulties created by multigrade instruction were nearly similar for each country. Differences primarily related to financial, geographic, and demographic variables.

Multigrade classes in these countries tend to have large numbers of students and few teachers. The most common pattern of organization is the two-grade combination class. However, three or more grades per classroom were common to all countries. Of the eight countries represented, none indicated they had "single-grade" schools with more than four grades. For example, an individual teacher may have a classroom of 30 fourth-graders and 27 fifth-graders or a classroom of 35 students in grades 3-6. Teachers in these situations face a formidable teaching situation.

During the conference, five general problem areas emerged:

1. *Inadequately trained teachers*
2. *Scarcity of varied levels and types of materials*
3. *Lack of flexible and special types of curriculum organization for multigrade classes*
4. *Inadequate school facilities*
5. *Lack of incentives for teachers of multiple classes*

Similar to preservice training in the United States, all countries participating in the conference reported that the teacher preparation for working in multigrade classrooms was identical to that provided for teachers of single-grade classrooms. In other words, individuals going into teaching were not prepared for teaching multigrade classrooms. Ironically, the concerns and depiction of problems in these developing countries echo many of the concerns voiced in the United States and Canada by multigrade classroom teachers and rural educators.

The most prominent similarities are the need for curriculum and program modifications that reflect the culture of the local community, and the needs of students within the demands created by the multigrade organization. In this regard, two recommendations emerged from the conference.

First, curriculum needs to be restructured so that it is community based. UNESCO concluded that the environment in which the community lives, the history and culture, and the utilization of skilled The qualitative studypersons in the community for improving the quality of education should be emphasized.

Second, innovative programs have a difficult time because the existing educational system is traditional, and this constrains perceptions of what may be possible. According to UNESCO, the four walls of the classroom and the long periods demanded by programs in different countries somewhat inhibit and restrict the child's activities. Outdoor activities should be encouraged and experiences outside the classroom should be given a place in the curriculum.

Currently, the Education and International Development (EID) Group at the Institute of Education, London University, is carrying out research designed to raise awareness among policymakers, planners, and practitioners of the extent, problems, and needs of the multigrade teaching and learning environment.

Currently, Peru has approximately 21,500 primary multigrade schools, 96 percent of which are located in rural areas. In terms of teachers, 41,000 teach in rural primary schools with multigrade classrooms, representing 69 percent of the total rural teaching force. Most of the schools in the countryside are multigrade, which testifies to the importance of this type of school for improving the educational level of the rural population. Among the most important characteristics affecting education are:

— *The dispersion and isolation of the rural population.*

— *The poverty of the villages (60 percent of the population in rural areas are poor and 37 percent live in situations of extreme poverty).*

— *The family economy, which requires and includes children's work, as members of the family.*

— *Linguistic and cultural diversity. However, despite this diversity, the language of school is Spanish, and bilingual education programs have very limited coverage.*

— *In rural areas children begin school late, have a high rate of repetition, have periodic interruptions in their studies, and so forth, all of which increases the heterogeneity of the multigrade class.*

The schools have severe deficiencies in infrastructure, access to services, availability of classroom furniture, equipment, and materials for teaching, and educational support. The teachers live in precarious conditions (no electricity, pure water, furniture, or adequate space in which to prepare their classes or to cook food); they have scarce incentives (a bonus of $13 per month), and scarce support and attention from high-level offices.

Formal teacher training does not instruct teachers in multigrade methodology, and often teachers do not speak the students' language. Multigrade teaching in Sri Lanka is common. It is common in rural and plantation schools where there are very few human and physical resources. A range of reasons for multigrade teaching could be identified in the Sri Lankan context, the most significant reason being nonavailability of one teacher per grade in these schools.

The difficulty in access, sparse pupil populations that restrict the appointment of one teacher per grade, and difficult living conditions are the major factors contributing to teacher scarcity. Most of these schools have student numbers ranging from 50 to 150. According to the latest school census data by the Ministry of Education, there are 1,252 schools out of the 10,120 schools in Sri Lanka that have fewer than three teachers. Even the schools in urban areas face the challenge of organizing the teaching-learning situations similar to a multigrade setting during some parts of the day or during some days for various reasons.

In Sri Lanka, the national primary school curriculum is organized toward teaching in single-grade schools. Teachers in multigrade classrooms face the difficulty of organizing the national curriculum to suit their teaching and learning needs. Teachers are not given training to address such situations, as there is no provision in the teacher education curriculum for multigrade teaching methodology. Thus, the teaching in these schools is of very low quality. The student dropout rate is very high in these schools.

Since the 1980s, the Department of Primary Education has attempted to try out multigrade teaching strategies in some selected schools under the UNICEF-assisted program for quality development of primary education. Very little research has been conducted on multigrade teaching in Sri Lanka.

There are many forms of multigrade classes in Vietnam, with two, three, four, or five different levels in any one class. So far, multigrade schools are quite widely used in ethnic minority areas with the purpose of providing primary education to disadvantaged children by bringing schools closer to communities where children live.

Currently there are 2,162 primary schools with multigrade classes, accounting for 1.8 percent of total primary schools, and there are 143,693 students learning in multigrade classes, accounting for 1.38 percent of the school population. Some problems include:

— *There is a serious shortage of teachers, especially skilled teachers for multigrade teaching.*

— *Teachers of multigrade classes are working in difficult and isolated conditions.*

— *The training of teachers for multigrade classes does not meet the requirement in either quality or quantity.*

— *Teaching methods of the ethnic minority schools are very poor and unsuccessful. Students are not encouraged to be involved actively in the teaching-learning process.*

— *Most of the multigrade schools lack textbooks, guidebooks, and reference materials for students and teachers. Teaching equipment is very simple. Many multigrade classes are in very bad condition.*

— *Pupils face language barriers in learning and regular interruption in their education.*

Many affective gains have also been documented in multigrade research. Students show increased self-esteem, more cooperative behaviour, better attitudes toward school in general, increased pro-social (caring, tolerant, patient, supportive) behaviour, enriched personal relationships, increased personal responsibility, and a decline in discipline problems. Older students in particular develop mentoring and leadership skills as a result of serving as role models and helping the younger children.

Overall on mental health and school attitudes, 52 percent of the studies indicated multigrade schools were better for students. Forty-three percent indicated single and multigrade schools had a similar influence on students. Only 5 percent found multigrade worse than graded schools. Students in multigrade schools were more likely to have positive self-concept, high self-esteem, and good attitudes toward school than students in single-grade classrooms. On mental health measures, students from multigrade settings felt more positive or the same as graded students.

After five years in one multigrade, open-space program, significantly fewer multigrade students were referred for discipline in junior high school. Underachievers in multigrade schools had better self-concept, attitudes toward school, and academic achievement than underachievers in graded schools.

Students of lower socioeconomic status also showed greater academic achievement when placed in multigrade schools. Kathleen Cotton, a researcher funded by the U.S. Department of Education's Office of Educational Research and Improvement, researched Longitudinal studies At-risk studentsseveral educational studies in regard to developmentally appropriate practice and multigrade education. This included a 1993 analysis of 46 documents. Cotton pointed out that most of the studies found that achievement in multigrade classrooms appeared to be no different than achievement in a single-grade classroom. The big differences were in attitude, behaviour, social skill development, leadership skills, and parental attitudes. The studies that Cotton looked at all pointed to the multigrade classroom as providing significantly more positive outcomes.

In addition, Cotton found that multigrade arrangements lend themselves to integrated curriculum, cooperative learning, cross-age tutoring, and learning in a more naturalistic setting.

Variation in grades, time of year, quality of instruction, and socioeconomic status, to mention only a few key variables, mediate student perceptions. Educational researchers studying student attitudes often have difficulty setting up studies where these variables can be adequately controlled. One compensating strategy is the aggregation of studies across setting and time. Practitioners can have greater confidence when many studies indicate similar results.

Viewed as a whole, the studies presented clearly indicate that students in multigrade classrooms tend to have significantly more positive attitudes toward themselves and school. A trend toward more positive social relationships is also indicated. Clearly, these studies indicate that being a student in a multigrade classroom does not negatively affect academic performance, student social relationships, or attitudes.

In terms of academic achievement, the data clearly support the multigrade classroom as a viable and equally effective organizational alternative to single-grade instruction. When it comes to student affect, the case for multigrade organization appears much stronger, with multigrade students outperforming single-grade students in more than 75 percent of the measures used. One wonders, then, why we do not have more schools organized into multigrade classrooms.

In general, teachers are said to prefer single grades because multigrade classes mean more planning, preparation, organization, and work; catering to a wider range of abilities and maturity levels; less time for meeting individual student needs and for remediation; less time for reflection on teaching; lack of relevant professional training; and less satisfaction with their work.

Some positive perceptions have been identified. These usually concern students' social skill development, opportunities for the enhancement of learning by the lower grade-level group through exposure to upper grade-level work, reinforcement of earlier learning for the upper grade-level students, and opportunities for children to learn through peer tutoring. Parent perceptions are also reported to be negative in general, though more so in urban as opposed to rural communities.

The chief parental concern is said to be about the level of student achievement. One of the reasons principals prefer to have single grades is the degree of parental concern about multigrade classes and the time and energy spent in dealing with those concerns. The chief disadvantages perceived by principals were the necessity for teachers to prepare two curricula, the strength of parental concerns, and the negative attitude of teachers. The advantages mentioned emphasized administrative ease in coping with student numbers, but also included comments about social skill development and learning from peers.

Radical change is a difficult and often messy process, an observation well-documented by the education change literature. With increased professional development, primary teachers made many positive changes in the early years. They were hampered, however, by uneven implementation timelines and lack of guidance from a state department undergoing reorganization.

The multigrade program was implemented on schedule but without some of the supports built into the law. For instance, in three schools, the multigrade program was well under-way before family resource centres were established. The extended school services program was available early on, but in most of the study schools it was offered only to students in the fourth or higher grades.

The changes in multigrade classrooms have not been readily accepted by all teachers. Many teachers feared that movement away from the traditional, teacher-directed scope-and-sequence approach to instruction would result in the young students learning less. Parents and teachers often remarked that students coming out of the multigrade programs had weak spelling skills and hadn't memorized their math facts.

Changes in multigrade classrooms have been substantial, but movement toward greater implementation of the program has slowed considerably in the study schools. Generally, multigrade teachers seem to have settled into an approach comfortable for them, whether it equates to multigrade program implementation or not. The reasons vary from one school to the next. Four factors are prevalent at most schools:

(1) *emphasis on the critical attributes rather than on the overall purpose of the multigrade program,*

(2) *legislative adjustments to the multigrade program,*

(3) *lack of perceived fit between the multigrade program and results-based reform in grades 4-12, and*

(4) *questions of efficacy, linked to teacher belief systems.*

At the same time that primary teachers were struggling to figure out how to implement the multigrade program and why they should do so, legislative changes influenced program implementation. The unintended effect of the new timeline adopted in 1992, coupled with the educational goals becoming statutory requirements, was that teachers were thrust into the overwhelming demands of multigrade classrooms before the state provided them with curriculum guidance.

They had received ample training in new instructional approaches, but had little time to reflect on them and figure out how to weave challenging content into multigrade settings in ways to help students learn. The result was that primary teachers worked feverishly to fashion a program that demonstrated implementation of the goals, but, under the surface, many fundamental issues-such as the program's philosophy and how the curriculum should align-had not been worked out.

The teachers studied were experiencing difficulty by the 1993-94 school year, their second year of multigrade program implementation. Teachers doubted the new methods they were using. They feared students might not be learning the basics, now that many primary teachers no longer relied on textbooks as the main curriculum and no clear curriculum had emerged to replace them.

At the same time, primary teachers were under pressure from some parents who did not understand the new ways of reporting and from intermediate teachers who reported that students were coming to them unable to work independently and without mastery of important basic skills. Multigrade teachers were also struggling to manage a wide range of abilities and age levels in their classrooms, often without knowing how or appreciating the purpose of doing so.

Thus, multigrade teachers had reached a point by the end of the 1993-94 school year where they strongly needed a boost of some sort if they were to push forward toward greater multigrade implementation. In the multigrade program, the focus had been on eliminating student failure and on building student self-esteem and love of learning. This was accomplished through mandates about how multigrade classrooms should operate.

In all the study schools, educators have arrived at a comfortable mix of innovative and traditional practices, although the mix is different from school to school. Four factors were influential in the development of the multigrade program at the local level: principal leadership, teacher beliefs, school climate, and the school's performance on the state assessment program. At some schools, these factors facilitated innovation in the multigrade program; at others, the factors operated in ways that hindered implementation.

The principal's ability to foster a common vision among the faculty and to build a supportive environment was a key factor in how multigrade programs were implemented. Stability was also important, with frequent changes in principals undermining school improvement, even when individual principals were strong. Whether or not teachers shared common beliefs about multigrade education, and what those beliefs were, strongly influenced the development of a school's multigrade program.

Where teachers were united in their approach to the multigrade program and in having high expectations for students, the program generally appeared successful, whether the school was implementing the letter of the law or not. If teachers held widely varying beliefs, they had difficulty developing a common commitment to a primary program that might contribute to overall school improvement.

School climate refers to the general atmosphere of and mood at the school, including relations between teachers and administrators, camaraderie among staff and faculty, expectations for students, and attitude toward parents. In the study schools, a variety of situations producing positive school climates were observed. These included a tradition of academic excellence; strong principal leadership willingly accepted by teachers, students, and parents; "laissez-faire" principal oversight combined with strong teacher leadership; and active parent support or passive acceptance by parents of what the school was doing.

Schools with less positive school climates exhibited characteristics such as poor relations between the principal and teachers and lack of camaraderie among teachers. In such schools, it was difficult for the faculty to maintain coordinated, consistent efforts to improve education. In some of the studies, the educators and parents alike support a traditional approach, have had success with it, and are unlikely to change that approach.

In other schools, local conflicts and leadership issues have hindered the development of consistency in instructional approaches. Some of the national researchers involved with previous multigrade primary programs have addressed the philosophical issue that is seen at work in the study schools.

Multigrade teachers must be able to facilitate positive group interaction and to teach social skills and independent learning skills to individual students. The critical judgment and common sense of teachers are essential ingredients in successful implementation. Methods that sound promising in theory may need considerable adaptation to be effective in practice.

Ideally, teachers should have opportunities to observe competent models demonstrating multigrade methods, try them out in the classroom, receive feedback on their efforts, reflect on the experience, revise their plans, and try again. Administrators should understand the principles underlying multigrade organization and developmentally appropriate instructional practices. In planning for implementation, however, knowledge about the change process may be even more valuable. Innovations often fail because policymakers give teachers insufficient time, training, and psychological support. Effectively implementing a single innovation requires several years and multigrade teaching involves multiple, complex innovations.

Administrators must realize that many of the underlying assumptions of multigrade teaching conflict with deeply ingrained assumptions underlying traditional age-graded instructional methods. Miller observes that for many teachers, "unlearning powerfully held notions about how children learn" is an essential part of implementing multigrade practices. This process is demanding, even for the most receptive and flexible individuals.

Multigrade instructional and organizational skills differ greatly from those used in the single-grade classroom. Veterans may feel as insecure as first-year teachers as they struggle to learn these new skills. In one school, Miller found that teachers with more experience seemed to feel even greater frustration in the early stages of change. To help teachers weather this stressful transition process, administrators must provide psychological support as well as technical assistance.

They must create a school culture that supports teacher learning, an environment in which it is safe to risk making mistakes. Without such support, many teachers will retreat to safe, familiar, age-graded methods. The principal plays a key role in creating this supportive school culture. The principal must provide teachers with opportunities to learn multigrade teaching methods, monitor the progress of implementation, and give teachers praise, feedback, and suggestions. He or she should be adept at facilitating positive, cooperative interactions among teaching team members.

The principal must ensure that all teachers feel supported and endeavour to maintain a sense of community within the school. Innovative efforts by small groups of teachers can threaten to split teaching staff into "pro" and "con" subgroups; avoiding intra-school strife can resemble a delicate tightrope walk. The principal must also deal with teachers who are unwilling or unable to make the transition. Finally, the principal must build support for multiage practices in the larger community.

Facilitating this transition requires sophisticated leadership and interpersonal skills, as well as personal characteristics such as patience and empathy. But most administrators receive little or no formal training in these skills. Those who possess them have generally learned them from experience, says Fullan, Principals need opportunities for professional development and for interaction with colleagues who are facing similar challenges. They need support from district administrators as they develop these facilitative skills.

Sufficient time and money are essential ingredients in creating and maintaining the multigrade classroom. Multigrade teaching takes years to master, and long-term staff development is expensive. Effective multigrade teaching is more time-consuming than age-graded teaching. Teachers often donate immense amounts of unpaid personal time during implementation, but few can maintain such sacrifice on a long-term basis, nor should they be asked to. Administrators must accept the challenge of communicating to the public that educational quality cannot exist without adequate financial support, and enlist their aid in providing these resources.

Multigrade classroom instruction places greater demands on teachers than teaching in a single grade. To be effective, teachers need to spend more time in planning and preparation. This often means modifying existing grade-level materials to ensure that students will be successful. In addition, there are many demands that are simply conditions of rural life.

Although rural living can have many rewards, these demands, affect the rural teacher. When considered along with the requirements of the multigrade classroom, it is clear that the rural, multigrade classroom teacher has a demanding, but potentially very rewarding, job. If the combination classroom seems like a formidable challenge to most teachers, then the classroom or school that combines three or more grades must appear to be an insurmountable obstacle.

How can one teacher juggle all those grades, with their wide levels of student maturity, ability, and motivation? How can one teacher possibly prepare for the many curricular areas, meet individual student needs, and have the time to eat lunch? Teaching a broad range of grade levels in the same classroom is complex and demanding. But there are many successful teachers and students who are living proof that mixed-grade classes are a viable organizational structure for learning. Although empirical studies of these classrooms are quite scarce, enough descriptive literature has been compiled to illustrate both the complexity and the rewards of the multigrade classroom.

Several advantages accrued for children and their parents in this rural school. The observed positive qualities far outweighed the disadvantages, and, more importantly, the values emphasized in the school reflected the community's values. This match of values is rarely achieved in heterogeneous urban schools. Value congruence between home and school certainly fostered a secure, stable world for these children to grow up in. Clearly, Dodendorf 's study suggests that the five-grade classroom can be a socially and academically effective learning environment for students. The implication, however, is that success depends on the ability of the teacher to organize and manage instruction so that cooperation, independence, and a motivation to learn become environmental norms.

Students are given responsibility for a large share of housekeeping tasks on a rotating basis: keeping the room clean, taking care of paper and supplies, checking out books, ringing the bell, monitoring play equipment, organizing the calendar, leading the flag salute, and sharpening pencils. Each week a student is honoured by not having duties for the week. Developing self-reliance, responsibility, and independence in students enables the teacher to better meet individual student needs. It also develops a strong sense of community and cooperation within the classroom.

Students might also work together to complete tasks while the teacher meets with students individually. Reading, math, English, and spelling are handled in this individualized manner. All other subjects are taught as a group, with each student working at his or her particular level; art, social studies, science, and music projects are frequently employed. The entire school also sings together, plays recorders, has a marching band, and publishes a school newspaper. Because the school is so isolated, it serves as the center of the community. Parents provide help with track meets, field trips, and special programs.

In the lower-level class, the teacher organizes instruction around key concepts that can be introduced to all students and then individualized to the different levels in the class. Students were also grouped by ability so that the talented second-grader could work with the fourth-grader, or the slower student could work with younger students for special skills. The teachers have used a two-phased approach to group instruction. In the first phase, they introduced a concept to the entire class. This allowed for cross-grade interaction with the concurrent benefits of younger students learning from older ones. It also is a more efficient use of teacher time.

Special events such as holidays, field trips, or any activity that does not require strict grouping by ability (such as closed-task skills) are organized around total class participation. Every member of the class contributes and shares in the successes of everyone else. Students also learn to be responsible and self-directed, to work independently, to provide help to others, and to receive help when needed. This independence is critically important because it enables the teacher to work individually with students.

In terms of academic achievement, multigrade students do not appear to fare any better or worse than single-grade students. Some research evidence does suggest there may be significant differences depending on subject and/or grade level. Primarily, these studies reflect the complex and variable nature of school life. However, there are not enough of these studies to make safe generalizations regarding which subjects or grade levels are best for multigrade instruction.

The evidence drawn from research focusing on affective student measures provides a strong case supporting multigrade instruction. Student attitudes toward school and self tend to be more positive in the mixed-grade classrooms. Multigrade students also interact more with students of other ages and have more positive attitudes toward peers than single-grade students. Several factors appear to play a part in these differences. In the multigrade classroom, student developmental and academic differences can be handled more easily than in a single-grade class.

Multigrade students regularly interact with a wide range of students. This increases the likelihood that individual students can find an academic or developmental match in their class. For example, the immature upper-grade student may find a lower grade student to befriend without the stigma generally associated with "hanging around with younger students." In a similar manner, the teacher can have lower-performing students from an upper grade work with students in the lower grade without the burden associated with out-of-grade-level placement.

Students also learn the advantages inherent in behaving cooperatively with older and younger students, and they have a greater opportunity to develop responsibility by modelling and helping other students. On face value, students in multigrade classrooms would appear to be better off than students in a single-grade classroom. However, the evidence suggests that from the point of view of school organizational norms and levels of teacher preparedness, the multigrade classroom generally serves as a temporary remedy to school enrolment and financial concerns.

Managing the Classroom

Managing the classroom is a critical element in successful instruction and requires good organizational ability and consistency. Students come into the classroom expecting the teacher to give them guidance and direction about rules and procedures and how the classroom is organized for instructional use. Having a uniform and predictable set of rules and procedures simplifies the task of being successful.

Having clear and efficient routines makes classroom life run smoothly. Because there are so many differ-ent levels in a multigrade classroom, the need for clear, consistent rules and procedures is even more critical than in traditional, single-grade classrooms. Effective teachers have been consistently observed by researchers to engage in three distinct phases of classroom management and discipline:

(1) planning before school begins,

(2) implementing plans, and

(3) maintenance.

Each phase will be presented in this book, along with examples of what effective teachers do during each phase.

Phase 1: Preparing for the Beginning of School

Effective teachers make their expectations explicit through clear rules and procedures that are consistently taught and enforced. The first few weeks of school are used to establish these expectations. Therefore, early planning and preparation before school begins is critical for starting the school year right. As one multigrade teacher noted, "Teachers must have their own idea of what the classroom will look like and how it will function before the first day of school." In other words, before the students arrive, the teacher must develop a vision of classroom life: how students will behave and relate to one another, where they will work, how resources will be organized, and other important classroom considerations.

During Phase 1, teachers focus on planning the arrangement of the classroom, organizing supplies and materials, and planning instructional activities for the first few days of school. Effective teachers focus on organizing furnishings and materials in order to facilitate instruction in several general ways:

(1) *student seating should be easy to monitor by the teacher and not distracting to the students;*

(2) *well-used areas of the room should be easily accessible; and*

(3) *materials and equipment should be quite accessible by students and the teacher.*

Establishing productive norms for student behavior can make the difference between success and failure for a classroom teacher. These norms are best set early in the year in a variety of ways, such as "teacher praise for appro-priate behavior, corrective feedback, formally presented rules, establishing procedures that regulate behavior during classroom activities, and academic work requirements".

Students must learn how to behave in a wide variety of work and social situations. If the teacher can lay out in advance the desired expectations for some of these situations, it is more likely that students will behave in the desired manner. Some of the activities that must be planned for are:

— *Whole-class instruction*

— *Teacher-led small groups*

— *Independent, small, cooperative workgroups*

— *Individual seatwork*

— *Transitions between activities*

— *Room and equipment use*

— *Tutoring students*

— *Giving and receiving assignments*

Once a teacher develops clear expectations for student behavior in different learning and social areas, the next step is to decide on consequences for students who follow or do not follow these expectations. Consequences may be divided into two general areas: rewards and punishment. Stickers, awards, prizes, or privileges are examples of commonly used extrinsic rewards. When students are successful and receive teacher feedback, approval, and recogni-tion, the need for extrinsic rewards is minimal.

Students who have disabilities will break the rules like anyone else, and they should receive similar consequences. Student participation in creating the best learning environment will create a class that manages lessons and time well. As students become more capable and able to take on responsibility, they will want to voice their opinions on aspects of school life. Teachers should be able to listen to their ideas and implement them.

Phase 2: Beginning the School Year

During this phase, the teacher seeks to put into practice plans that have been developed prior to the start of school. This is the time when norms are established and students develop a view of how "their particular class will operate." Emmer identifies four principles that can help the teacher get off to a good start:

Teach rules and expectations as if they were academic content. For example, if you use cooperative workgroups, be sure students know what it looks like to cooperate and give them the opportunity to practice. Students should know from the teacher exactly what is expected for the different types of classroom activities. A recently completed five-year study of a program designed to teach elementary students prosocial behaviors demonstrated the effectiveness of treating rules and expectations as academic content.

Children in the program displayed more spontaneous prosocial behavior toward one another, and were more supportive, friendly, and helpful than students in a group of comparison schools. However, it was not only teaching desired social skills and behavior that produced the results, but also structuring the learning environment and teacher modeling. It is important to recognize that students may be anxious or nervous about their new environment. They may have concerns about being successful, getting along well with others socially, and doing the "right" thing.

Research has demonstrated that the most effective teachers maintain a highly central role in the classroom. They are not authoritarian tyrants, but they do not turn the class over to the students. They make decisions aimed at achiev-ing specific purposes, and they monitor their decisions for effectiveness. For example, if they want students to work in small problem-solving groups, they make sure students know how to work cooperatively and that the assignment is clearly understood.

Then they monitor group progress to ensure that students are successful in carrying out their assignment. It is important to teach students that how we act and interact with others is our own responsibility. As a teacher, maintain a positive classroom climate. All students must be taught how to interact with others and, of course, teachers must model respect for them with an impartial and caring attitude. No amount of teaching can overshadow our own actions and behavior. All students will benefit from a good role model, particularly in a teacher's interactions with students who have challenges.

Phase 3: Maintaining Good Discipline

Once the school year is underway and positive student social and academic norms have been established, the teacher must seek to maintain these norms. In this phase, the teacher's role shifts toward keeping high levels of student engagement and preventing disruptions of the learning environment. Emmer divides this phase into two key areas:

Effective teachers are good managers who do not ignore large amounts of inappropriate behavior. They monitor classroom norms continuously, stopping and then redirecting incidents of unacceptable behavior in a prompt and timely manner. However, these teachers are not negative or sarcastic toward student misbehavior, and they respond in ways that do not call attention to the problem at hand.

Students enjoy an environment that changes periodically. Study centers with pictures and color invite enthusiasm for your subject. Young people like to know about you and your interests. Include personal items in your classroom. A family picture or a few items from a hobby or collection on your desk will trigger personal conversations with your students. As they get to know you better, you will see fewer problems with discipline.

Just as you may want to enrich your classroom, there are times when you may want to impoverish it as well. You may need a quiet corner with few distractions. Some students will get caught up in visual exploration. For them, the splash and color act as a siren that pulls them off task. They may need more "vanilla" and less "rocky road." Have a place to which you can steer these youngsters. Let them get their work done first, then come back to explore and enjoy the rest of the room.

Most students are sent to the principal's office as a result of confrontational escalation. The teacher has called them on a lesser offense, but in the moments that follow, the student and the teacher are swept up in a verbal maelstrom. Much of this can be avoided when the teacher's intervention is quiet and calm.

An effective teacher will take care that the student is not rewarded for misbehavior by becoming the focus of attention. She moves around and monitors the activity in her classroom. She anticipates problems before they occur. Her approach to a misbehaving student is inconspicuous. Others in the class are not distracted.

Many different approaches have been used by teachers for storing and locating instructional materials. In the multigrade classroom, it is important that these materials be located and labeled so that students can function independently of the teacher. Often, in classrooms organized for individualized instruction, teachers organize materials into resource centers.

Some teachers have small groups of children make the mobiles as an art activity during the first few days of school. It is an easy way to involve students in setting up the room or area. In addition, clear labeling can reduce the demands students make on teachers for help.

Keeping daily attendance and the morning lunch count are a require-ment in most schools. Depending on the number of students, these can consume a small amount of time each day. Several suggestions follow that may increase teacher efficiency:

— *Prepare a dittoed class list. Students complete their own atten-dance sheet by drawing a self-portrait or making a check on the space by their name. For lunch count, students can mark an appropriate "yes" box for hot lunch or milk.*

— *If tote boxes are used, look at the names on boxes left on the shelf. These students should make up the absentee list.*

— *Set up an attendance lunch count board or pocket chart.*

Students whose names are left should make up the absentee list. An especially promising strategy for protecting instructional time during attendance and related managerial duties has been identified by a number of multigrade teachers. This popular strategy is the "entry task." When students first enter the classroom in the morning, after lunch, or any other time, they encounter an entry task written on the board.

In the morning before beginning instruction, some teachers set aside time for making announcements regarding the day's activities and special events. One of the problems that multigrade teachers face is providing individ-ual help for students while the teacher is engaged in tutoring or small-group instruction. A successful technique is to develop procedures that clearly spell out what is expected when one needs help and the teacher is busy.

These are called "help systems." Students need to understand that not being able to get immediate attention from the teacher is not an excuse to do nothing. Using a help system can reduce student dependency on the teacher and help build self-direction in students. Several help strategies have been found to be useful:

— *Have students use a sign-up system, as shown below, that enables them to be specific about the type of help needed. For example, you could have the following four areas on the chalkboard:*

— *Colored cones can be used to signal for help. The student puts a red cone in front of him and continues to work until you come to help. Different colors can stand for a different problem.*

— *Secure a two-colored tag to each desk or table. One side of the tag means "progressing alone" and the other indicates "help needed," or one color indicates an immediate need while the other color indicates a tutoring need that can be temporarily postponed.*

— *Larger, two-colored cards may be placed flat on the desks or in a folded "tepee" shape. When the student needs help the teacher can see this cue when scanning the room. Various colors can be used to indicate the need for different types of assistance.*

— *Use a card file system for locating peer tutors. File the students' names under the Subject Area on which they will tutor.*

Students who are to be "mini-teachers" should be asked to rehearse their methods of tutoring with you. They should understand that a tutor stresses the use of questioning (in contrast to telling), the use of diagrams or manipulative materials, and the use of verbal praise. One goal for students in the multigrade classroom is that they become involved in selecting and managing their own educational experiences. Successful multigrade teachers have found it critically important that students learn to manage their own time, make decisions, and evaluate what has been happening to them. Students who successfully manage their time tend to:

- *Bring only essential things to school*
- *Clean out cubicles, lockers, or tote boxes once a week*
- *Keep multigrade papers in a binder or folder*
- *Use a planning schedule to help them keep track of what to do Organizing Student Activities*

It is critically important to establish clear expectations for students if your class is to be successfully managed. Students need to know what you expect in simple but direct terms. In developing a set of guidelines for students, you may wish to involve them. This will help to develop student understanding, motivation, and ownership. However, it is essential that once a list is set up, students are taught the rules and then systematically monitored to determine how well they are working. When developing a list of classroom rules, it is helpful to begin with one's beliefs or principles about classroom behavior.

Multigrade Classroom: An Instructional Organisation

There is greater diversity of achievement and developmental levels in the multigrade classroom than in the typical single-grade classroom. This diversity creates a greater demand on teacher time. Therefore, teachers often find themselves having to rely more on students to work independently and to help one another than the single-grade teacher.

This means that students need to be self-directed, motivated, and responsible learners. They need to be able to help one another, set and complete learning goals, follow teacher directions, and stay on task with a minimum of teacher supervision. Observations of effective multigrade classrooms demonstrate that student behaviours such as independence, cooperation, and self-direction are essential for instructional success.

Instead, several models of instructional organization and evaluation and how they affect student performance will be introduced. These models will aid in determining how to organize classroom instruction and evaluation and analyzing the effect of this instruction on students. In addition, issues relating to scheduling instruction and sequencing curriculum will be presented.

In the multigrade classroom, teachers have successfully dealt with this problem by tailoring assignments to match the unique needs of each student and grouping students where common needs have been identified. If we had an ideal classroom, one where all students function at the same achievement level and exert a similar amount of effort, it would be easier for the teacher to effectively instruct all students at the same time with similar strategies and materials. However, in the real world, students vary considerably within most single-grade classrooms, and teachers are forced by necessity to deal with different ability levels.

In the multigrade environment, differences in ability are even more pronounced, requiring increased planning and organization. The most common strategies for handling differences in ability are whole-class instruction (where differences may often be ignored), ability grouping (where differences often become institutionalized), and pull-out programs (where students are removed from their regular classroom for specific subjects).

Student effort relates to the amount of perseverance and commitment a student brings to a learning task. In the typical

U.S. school, students begin in the primary grades believing that their performance and ability are a direct result of their effort. By the time a student reaches the sixth grade, effort, performance, and ability become reversed so that students believe ability is a capacity that affects effort and performance. Ability is viewed as a kind of fixed quantity that determines the degree to which effort can alter performance.

In other words, a "smart" student (one with high ability) gets good grades with minimal effort, while the "slow" student (one with low ability) puts out lots of effort with poor results. Consequently, the low-performing student is not motivated to try. The high-performing student believes that the good grade was deserved because he or she learned the material. The student who believes that increased effort will have no effect on one's ability to learn will likely be difficult to motivate.

The U.S. school as a place for learning helps to develop in students a belief that ability, not effort, is the key to success. Although it may not be a deliberate and premeditated strategy, the type of instructional organization utilized will directly affect student views of themselves as successful learners. Teachers organize instruction based upon their beliefs about student learning. These teacher expectations tend to be fulfilled by students, which in turn reinforces the teacher beliefs about student learning.

Thus, teachers' beliefs and understanding of the effects of instructional organization become crucial to the success of learning. Three patterns of instructional organization have been identified by Ames and Ames as contributing to student perceptions of themselves as learners. Recent research has focused on the goal structure of different types of instructional organization. Goal structure refers to the way in which instruction is organized to reward student performance. Three distinct methods of instructional organization have been identified and researched by Ames and Ames.

In this organizational structure students receive rewards on a competitive basis with their peers. In a typical competitive classroom, students are engaged in whole-class or small- or ability-group instruction. Learning tasks and activities are generally the same, with minor adjustments made for differences in ability. For example, during math instruction, all students are introduced to a concept and then given a seatwork assignment.

All students are likely to be working on identical assignments. Evaluation of student performance is a public activity where students have knowledge of how they performed in relation to their peers. Social comparison information is the primary cue for success.

Unlike competitive goal structures, an individualistic structure places a major emphasis on self-improvement. Students are individually rewarded for gains they make over past levels of performance. This type of organization is characterized by students working on individual learning programs tailored to their unique needs. Usually, some form of assessment has been given to each student. The results indicate areas where the student is performing below a given standard. When a student can achieve to the standard, he or she is rewarded with successful completion.

In this setting, it is likely that students would be working on different assignments and activities at the same time. Student success is based on individual comparisons with past and present performance, not on a comparison with other students. Cooperation is the third type of goal structure. It differs from both the competitive and individualistic patterns of organization because it emphasizes a positive interdependence among students for success or reward. Students depend on each other for task completion.

Some study demonstrates that cooperative strategies enhance student self-concept and motivation. Many teachers use cooperative learning strategies. In art class, the teacher might form the class into small groups in order to complete a group mural that depicts a theme in social studies. Less common are cooperative strategies used in academic areas such as reading and math. However, recent trends toward cooperative learning have generated a number of highly effective "packaged" training programs.

In many multigrade classrooms, teachers have learned to rely primarily on individualized and cooperative learning because they are natural out-growths of the way rural multigrade classrooms are organized. Students learn to cooperate and depend on one another and to work on tasks tailored to their individual needs. The teacher encourages and utilizes cooperation among students in order to extend learning. However, there is also a tendency to rely on competitive structures because they are the dominant educational practice beginning teachers learn.

Teachers faced with a classroom of students must learn to balance the needs of students with the time and energy necessary to meet those needs. A body of research on teaching and instructional organization describes practices and strategies that have proven effective in striking this balance. In so doing, this research has also illuminated a sobering reality that many instructional practices believed to be good for students may have undesirable effects on student efforts to learn.

In structuring the classroom for instruction, teachers nearly always use some form of grouping (the one exception may be a completely independent study program). Either they teach to the entire class (whole-group instruction), or they configure the class into different types of groups. For what purpose are different forms of group structure used?

Traditionally, grouping has served a management purpose in classrooms. In a similar fashion to the early evolution of the graded school, grouping has served as a means of sorting and organizing students into manageable units for efficiency purposes. An underlying belief is that instruction will be more effective with smaller numbers of students grouped by ability.

However, studies of ability grouping have clearly shown that the liabilities for low-achieving students may often be substantial and, except for mathematics, ability grouping does not appear to serve any advantage for students. The only exception may be in those cases where groups are temporarily formed for specific purposes such as peer editing. Bossert, Barnett, and Filby developed a model for describing the different patterns of instructional organization commonly found in schools along two continuums: activity structure and student work relationships.

A multidimensional/multiability classroom is one in which there are many dimensions of intellectual competence. No individual is likely to be treated highly on all these dimensions. Thus there are no students who are generally expected to be incompetent at new tasks and no students who are generally expected to be superior regardless of the nature of the task.

In a multidimensional/multiability classroom, one's skill in reading represents only one important competence; it is not an index of general expectations for success at all classroom tasks. In the multidimensional/multiability classroom, there is a shift in both student and teacher roles that is designed to increase learning opportunities and successes for all students. This is accomplished, in part, by changing and/or expanding instructional strategies to include cooperative work groups where students learn from each other and by increasing the array of areas where students can demonstrate competence.

Marshall and Weinstein identify four components of task or activity structure that enhance student self-perceptions and performance:

1. A *variety of tasks occur simultaneously:*

— *Variety in the tasks allows students to demonstrate their ability in several areas rather than along a single dimension. Variety allows students to feel competent in some areas. Conventional curriculum taps a very narrow range of skills, concentrating almost solely on reading and verbal skills, such as speaking and writing, yet rarely emphasizing alternative intellectual abilities in art, athletics, creativity, and thinking.*

— *Task variety reduces social comparison because evaluation is less visible.*

2. A *divergence in the process and products of the task:*

— *Divergent process is made up of tasks that can be pursued in a variety of ways.*

— *Divergent products have no specific right answers; results may be good in different ways. This allows for a variety of student experiences of success. Divergent tasks reduce the basis for comparative evaluation.*

3. *Differences exist in the sequence and pace of tasks for different individuals:*

— *Completion time requirements (pace) can harm the effects of divergent task activities if students are required to complete their tasks at the same time (i.e., those completing first are smarter).*

4. Level of task difficulty and content coverage varies:

— *Varying the amount of content and the difficulty of content for different students can communicate comparative evaluation information.*

— *Comparison can be reduced if the teacher conveys the belief that everyone is learning, but at different paces and in different ways.*

— *Teacher expectations of ability tend to convey a belief that ability level determines the quality and quantity of tasks assigned. When this is made public, students internalize the values and judge their own ability.*

In the multi-grade setting, the need to balance teacher time and efficiency with the best interest of students is a continual struggle. In other words, interdependency, cooperation, multiple task activities, individualized learning, and heterogeneous grouping appear to have emerged out of the requirements of coping with multiple grade levels in a single room. Recent research on effective teaching and instructional organization strategies describe classroom practices that appear to consistently counteract these forces.

Several factors play a role in determining whether an organizational structure (whole-class, small-group, etc.) enhances student learning. Teacher awareness of effective teaching practices and the ability to apply them to different organizational structures can overcome some of the inherent limitations of a particular structure. For example, in whole-class instruction there is a tendency to call on those students who are the brightest (selective attention).

This reduces the opportunity to learn for slower and average students. An effective teacher might allow for cooperative student responses (students respond in pairs), request responses from a wide variety of students, give students time to think before they answer (wait time), or have every student write out a response. Other examples that are especially relevant to the multigrade environment are the characteristics of the learning activities and the grouping structure used to apply them.

Effective strategies have been implemented to counteract the negative effects of organizing instruction along a single-ability dimension. Both students and teachers are trained to view ability as multifaceted, not a fixed entity possessed by only a few. In the traditional single-ability classroom, reading is generally viewed as a prerequisite for all other tasks.

Few activities are offered where other forms of ability, such as reasoning, decision-making, idea development, and observational skill, can be tested and verified. Cohen identifies three key areas for altering unidimensional classroom structure in order to change student and teacher views of intelligence and ability: increasing learning opportunities, increasing opportunities for success, and changing evaluation practices.

In larger districts and schools, all curriculum levels, from philosophy to assessment, are often clearly defined. The single-grade teacher in a metropolitan school district would likely be required to follow a specified set of goals and learning objectives while using district-adopted materials and tests. Multigrade teachers, on the other hand, may often find themselves in the role of answering these questions with little guidance from a central school district or governmental agency.

Even in those cases where the state or a central

educational service district provides guidance for the multi-grade school, isolation and small size will often reduce the amount of direct service. Even more confounding, curriculum goals, guides, and texts are conventionally organized by "grade level," placing the teacher in the dilemma of how to achieve expected learning goals when the instructional organization may well be inappropriate. Rural multigrade teachers often find themselves operating on their own.

When a teacher enters a classroom with a new group of students, the teacher's most pressing concern generally revolves around determining what the students already know and what they may need to learn. Ideally, there should be student records that provide an overview of individual student progress. These generally include standardized achievement test results, report cards, and diagnostic testing information for reading and math programs. However, this type of information is not often kept systematically.

In addition, if students are returning from a summer vacation, they may have regressed from the previous year's testing. Using grade-level placement information gathered from student records, as well as other information sources (such as colleagues or the community), plan lessons for diagnostic purposes. These might include writing activities, completing a series of math problems, or individually reading to the teacher.

When planning for diagnosis, it is important to set curricular priorities. If the district has established learning goals or adopted a curriculum, then these can be used to guide your decisions. However, if there do not appear to be any established guidelines, then you should use what classroom resources you can find and work with community members to help identify goals they have for their children.

There are many curriculum guides developed by state

departments of education that may be obtained by contacting them directly or by using ERIC (Educational Resources Information Center) to find curriculum guides and curriculum models. Finally, do not forget to use your own common sense to decide what the students need to learn.

The following guidelines provide an outline of ideas for collecting and assessing curriculum materials:

1.Determine what the school has that you can use:

— *Workbooks*

— *Worksheet masters*

— *Textbooks (old or new)*

— *Idea/activity books*

— *Learning kits*

— *Any type of hands-on materials*

2. *Determine whether there is any discretionary money for buying materials*
3. *Ask other school personnel what resources may be available*
4. *Check the local library for books, magazines, and Internet sites that will go with units of study*
5. *Examine teachers' manuals and note worksheets, games, devices, or other suggested learning activities*
6. *Collect materials that may be of use (such as magazines, maps, wallpaper books, carpet squares, milk cartons, etc.)*
7. *Look for simulations, games, and other social/ interactive learning activities, especially in social sciences*

Ideas about evaluation in multigrade classrooms rest on several premises. The first is that if students and teachers remain together for several years, teachers are able to ascertain what students know and do not know well, how they learn, and the best ways to teach them. The second premise is that if students progress through the curriculum less restrained by chronological age, then evaluation should accommodate their current knowledge and their need to grow.

Evaluation systems should track students' long-term learning within and across subject areas. This entails multilevel assessments, informal and formal peer modelling by older students, and challenging activities and assessments. The goal of spiral evaluation is to examine long-term learning over a three-year span. There are two ways in which evaluation "spirals." First, there is an upward spiral toward more conceptual complexity. Second, by revisiting certain aspects of the curriculum each year, students will experience long-term learning. By using spiral evaluation, teachers and students know what has been taught and learned over a three-year time span. There are three years to work toward transfer of concepts, information, and skills to new situations.

Spiral evaluation also has a positive impact on students' sense of security and the development of leadership. "Old" students (seventh- and eighth-graders) can explain a concept from the prior year to "new" students (sixth-graders).

For example, older students this fall explained to the incoming sixth-graders the multiple purposes of Agri-habitat and demonstrated how to work in the gardens. The old ones felt comfortable sharing what they had learned. They were mentoring at the same time that they were reviewing and determining what they knew.

Multigrade, multiyear, interrelated curriculum also means

that learning should be evaluated across the curriculum. Teachers should conceive of their curriculum and the evaluation of student learning as a "web" that crosses the hall from classroom to classroom. The web unites teachers in a common effort to secure student understanding in many contexts. For example, writing skills are evaluated across the curriculum in every subject area.

Spelling words in language arts are taken from other subjects, and examples of sentences for learning new writing skills are taken from social studies texts. Math word problems frequently relate to information from social studies and science.

The bridge represents a means of understanding students' perspectives; we are trying to evaluate what students believe they are learning, and how they are learning, over the three-year program. Bridges to student understandings are built on day-to-day interaction. Bridges are also erected through the systematic collection and analysis of research data.

Learning from assessment requires the willingness and the courage to examine your own effectiveness. It especially matters to a multigrade team that they know how to spiral, web, and bridge assessment practices. Students' academic shortcomings cannot be blamed on some other anonymous teacher; for three years multigrade teachers are responsible.

Peer Tutoring

Peer tutoring is cooperation between two or more students, where one individual imparts knowledge to the other(s). This can occur between students of the same age or grade (same-age tutoring) or between students of different ages or grades (cross-age tutoring). For example, when one student helps another student to learn math facts, we can say peer tutoring has taken place. This may be a sixth-grade student helping a first-grader or two first-graders tutoring each other.

In the traditional single-grade classroom, peer tutoring may occur on an incidental basis as when one student seeks help with a math problem from his or her neighbour. In the multigrade classroom, this incidental tutoring is an encouraged and necessary instructional activity. Research evidence specifically focusing on incidental tutoring in multigrade classrooms is nonexistent.

However, research on structured tutoring programs is abundant and overwhelmingly positive. Therefore, greater emphasis will be placed on structured tutoring. In addition, information collected from interviews and discussions with multigrade teachers supports the belief that underlying successful incidental tutoring are principles of effective instructional practice.

In the multigrade classroom, peer tutoring provides the teacher with a powerful strategy for extending the teacher's instructional influence. When teaching two or more different grades in a single classroom, especially when class size pushes above 15 students, the teacher may have difficulty directly responding to individual student needs. Multigrade teachers reporting on their experiences with peer tutoring indicated a strong dependence on students helping one another.

In nearly all reports, teachers indicated peer tutoring occurred on an incidental basis. That is, tutoring was not generally a systematically planned activity. Multigrade teachers indicated that peer tutoring need "not be planned in the sense of being written in the plan book, but is part of a good teacher's mental arsenal of methods to help students." It is worth noting that these teachers each had several years of experience in the multigrade classroom. As successful multigrade teachers, they learned through experience to capitalize on the capabilities of their students to help one another.

Seven different uses of peer tutoring in their classrooms were identified:

1. *Drill each other-spelling, math, and so forth.*
2. *Help other students develop a skill that the tutor possesses*
3. *Build self-esteem of the tutor*
4. *Peer modelling of skills-pushups, songs, dancing, and so forth.*
5. *Ask a student to explain a concept in "kid language"*
6. *Let a student (or students) teach a chapter in social studies*
7. *Help each other with study skills and researching*

In addition, the teachers identified a set of instructions that would be helpful for the tutor to follow:

— *Smile.*

— *Be friendly.*

— *Speak clearly.*

— *Keep your voice to a whisper or whatever volume is appropriate.*

Although the incidental tutoring described by the multigrade conference participants was described as "spontaneous" and "not something placed in the teacher's lesson plan book," it still has an element of structure. But the structure is based on years of classroom experience, where the teacher operates from a "good teacher's mental arsenal of methods to help students."

In other words, these teachers are able to match the needs of different students and apply an appropriate tutoring strategy in a spontaneous manner. However, when novice teachers enter the multigrade classroom, they generally do not have the advantage of years of experience. For these teachers, research-based guidelines for tutoring may prove to be valuable. Several features of peer tutoring have the greatest effect on student achievement and attitude.

1. *Structured tutoring is more effective than tutoring on an incidental basis.*
2. *Tutoring of shorter (zero to four weeks) duration appears to produce the best results. When tutoring continues past four weeks, there is a diminishing return.*
3. *Tutoring where lower level skills are taught and tested produces the best student outcomes.*
4. *Greater results occur in math, followed by reading, than in other subject areas.*

In using these results, remember that these conditions should not be viewed too narrowly or as absolutely necessary for successful peer tutoring. A large body of research on tutoring suggests that any organized and focused tutoring program will likely have a positive impact on student learning. The type of tutoring program used should always be closely monitored to determine if desired changes in the learner are occurring and, if not, the likely causes.

Because rural multigrade classrooms are often more informal than single-grade classrooms, tutoring activities may be implemented in a less structured, more spontaneous way. Children have certain advantages over adults in teaching peers. They may more easily understand tutees' problems because they are cognitively closer. Allen and Feldman found that third- and sixth-graders were more accurate than experienced teachers in determining from nonverbal behaviour whether agemates understood lessons.

The fact that their "cognitive framework" is similar may also help peer tutors present subject matter in terms their tutees understand. Peer tutors can effectively model study skills such as concentrating on the material, organizing work habits, and asking questions. Cohen notes that similarity between model and learner increases the influence of modelling. An at-risk child may more easily identify with a student relatively close in age, particularly one of the same ethnic or social background, than with an adult.

Higher status also promotes the effect of modelling. Cross-age tutoring takes advantage of the higher status inherent in the age difference while still retaining considerable similarity. Tutors who have struggled academically may be more patient and understanding than those who haven't. Empathy contributes greatly to low achievers' effectiveness as cross-age tutors. Tutors often "pick up on things teachers weren't able to" because they experienced similar problems a few years earlier.

. Tutors may also experience higher cognitive gains. Organizing material to teach "facilitates long-term retention, as well as aiding in the formation of a more comprehensive and integrated understanding". Tutoring also provides opportunities to practice and improve communication skills and work habits. Tutors' self-esteem rises as they see their tutees improve.

Knowing they are making a meaningful contribution is a powerful experience. Many tutors stop skipping classes and behaving disruptively after they realize they are role models for their tutees. Simply putting two students together won't result in successful tutoring. Untrained tutors, whether adults or students, may resort to threats of punishment and scornful put-downs. Tutors need training to master effective tutorial and communication skills.

Another potential problem is that student tutors may not

completely understand the material to be taught. Cohen suggests assessing potential tutors' comprehension before assigning them to tutor. However, a tutor need not be an excellent student, especially in the case of cross-age tutoring. The design of a tutoring program is dictated by its objectives, including the targeted age group and subject area, and by the availability of human, physical, and financial resources. Establishing specific, measurable objectives permits assessment of individual progress and evaluation of the program's success as a whole.

Frequent assessment of student progress gives program staff feedback on the effectiveness of lessons and encourages both tutor and tutee. Procedures must be established for selecting and matching tutors and tutees. Examples of tutee selection criteria include test scores and teacher judgment. Tutors may be screened for desired attitudes or levels of academic competence. The Valued Youth Program, which recruits students who meet state at-risk criteria, accepts those with records of minor disciplinary problems but draws the line at criminal behaviour.

Tutors also may be given basic training to accompany carefully structured materials, as in the Companion Reading Program, or extensive training that enables them to make more independent decisions. Extensive training is desirable when tutor progress is the main objective. Tutors need ongoing supervision and support. Younger tutors will require more structure and closer supervision.

Support by teachers and administrators is essential for a tutoring program to succeed in the long run. Foot, et al., list typical problems and concerns and recommend openly discussing them beforehand. Parents and the community should also be informed. Teachers who understand and believe in a program's potential to help their children will generally be firm supporters. Decades of research have established that well-planned peer tutoring programs can improve student achievement and self-esteem as well as overall school climate.

The wide variety of programs available should enable every interested school district to find a format that suits its needs. The design of a tutoring program is dictated by its objectives, including the targeted age group and subject area, and by the availability of human, physical, and financial resources. Establishing specific, measurable objectives permits assessment of individual progress and evaluation of the program's success as a whole. Frequent assessment of student progress gives program staff feedback on the effectiveness of lessons and encourages both tutor and tutee.

Procedures must be established for selecting and matching tutors and tutees. Examples of tutee selection criteria include test scores and teacher judgment. Tutors may be screened for desired attitudes or levels of academic competence. The Valued Youth Program, which recruits students who meet state at-risk criteria, accepts those with records of minor disciplinary problems but draws the line at criminal behaviour.

Tutors also may be given basic training to accompany carefully structured materials, as in the Companion Reading Program, or extensive training that enables them to make more independent decisions. Extensive training is desirable when tutor progress is the main objective. Tutors need ongoing supervision and support.

Younger tutors will require more structure and closer supervision. In periodic group meetings, older tutors gain psychological support by talking about frustrations and sharing success stories. Tutors can learn from each other's experiences as well as from staff suggestions for handling problems.

Support by teachers and administrators is essential for a

tutoring program to succeed in the long run. Foot, et al., list typical problems and concerns and recommend openly discussing them beforehand. Parents and the community should also be informed. Teachers who understand and believe in a program's potential to help their children will generally be firm supporters. Decades of research have established that well-planned peer tutoring programs can improve student achievement and self-esteem as well as overall school climate. The wide variety of programs available should enable every interested school district to find a format that suits its needs.

Before a tutoring program is implemented, six important question areas need to be reviewed and answered. Without some idea of where you want to go and how you plan to get there, your chances of ever arriving are slim. Successful peer tutoring may have positive effects on many different areas at the same time, but the important thing is to be clear on your primary purpose for using tutoring. Begin planning your tutoring program by writing down a few goals you would like to achieve.

To help you write your own tutoring goals, several examples follow:

— *Peer tutoring will be used in my classroom to increase achievement and on-task time in math for first- and second-graders*

— *Peer tutoring will be used during oral reading to increase student fluency and motivation*

— *Peer tutoring will be used to help students perform better on spelling quizzes*

Notice that each goal consists of two common elements: (1) who will receive the tutoring (first-and second-graders, all reading students, those performing poorly), and (2) what the tutoring will focus on (math achievement, on-task time, reading fluency, motivation, and poor spelling performance). In deciding your goals, be sure to include these two elements.

Equally important is establishing specific objectives (learner outcomes) for each tutoring pair or group that can be easily assessed. In organizing your classroom for tutoring, you need to consider what else will be going on during tutoring. If you choose to have tutoring occur in pairs during reading time, then the entire room might become a tutoring zone.

However, if you have students of several ages in your room at once and you want older students to tutor younger students in math, you may need to designate a special area for tutoring. Which curriculum area you choose will be guided by your knowledge of student needs, available materials and, ultimately, the success of the tutor. Generally, there are two possible directions you may choose. First, you may choose to focus on an academic content area such as math, where the tutor helps a student learn basic addition facts or assists the teacher in reinforcing how to add numbers. Or you may choose to focus on open-ended learning, where the tutor provides help to younger students who may need a combination of supervision and tutoring in order to complete an activity.

For example, if the teacher asks the primary grades to complete a series of plant activities in science that include planting a seed, collecting and labelling leaves, and making a plant scrapbook, older students might help the primary children in completing these tasks. The difference between academic content and open-ended learning centres on the openness of the tasks. In the first case there are clearly right and wrong answers, while in the second case the end results may be quite different for each student.

In addition, open-ended learning places greater emphasis

on supervision and support than does a focus on convergent academic tasks. Evaluation is an essential part of tutoring. How will you know if you have achieved your goals unless you have some form of assessment? Your evaluation should reflect your program goals. If you said you wanted to use peer tutoring to increase student fluency and motivation in reading, how would you know if this goal had been achieved? Do students who received tutoring read more fluently now than when they began tutoring? Do they act more motivated by checking out more books, volunteering to read during oral reading activities, or choosing reading during free time?

The following list will provide you with some possible sources of information to help you assess the effect tutoring has had in your classroom:

— *Interview learners*

— *Review textbook testing materials*

— *Observe learners and note changes in behaviour*

— *Standardized testing*

— *Talk to the tutor*

— *Talk to parents*

— *Make up a test or use workbook pages*

Peer tutoring has been shown to improve student performance for the tutor and the learner in a number of important areas such as self-esteem, academics, and motivation. In the multigrade classroom, tutoring has a history of extending the teachers' instructional influence. However, tutoring often appears to be a rather spontaneous, informal activity. Information presented by multigrade conference participants indicates both purpose and structure.

Because there are so many time demands placed on

multigrade teachers, it is critically important to remember to keep it simple and collect only what you need in order to make decisions regarding program change.

4

Educational Facilities in India

Educational Development Index (EDI) is proposed to be developed separately for rural and urban areas. Parameters required for the development of EDI are the same for both the areas (rural and urban). However, the percentage of population having schools within a prescribed distance is required for rural areas and not for the urban areas. Literacy is an output parameter to study the level of development of education in an area. Input parameters in the context of educational development indicates the efforts made in establishing and developing an education system whereas the output parameters are the outcome of these efforts.

Number of Schools, adult literacy centres, teachers, infrastructural facilities, investments in education - are few such input parameters and literacy, enrolment are few illustrative output parameters of education. The input parameters indicate the adequacy or inadequacy of developmental efforts wherein the output parameters are the indicators of the success or efficiency of the system thus established. Input parameters are the cost accrued for educational development and the output parameters are the benefits from the system. Literacy levels in

India, varies sharply across various regions, locations and among different sections of population, like Scheduled Castes and Scheduled Tribes.

In India, most of the states are located in high male and medium female literacy rate zone in urban areas. Four states viz, Assam, Himachal Pradesh, Maharashtra and Kerala are in the high male and high female literacy zone in urban areas. By 1997, there was major shift in the literacy level of male and female in rural areas and marginal shift in gender disparities in urban areas also. In 1997, there were eight states in male (high) and female (high / medium) category in rural areas in place of two states in this category in 1991. In urban areas also four out of the twelve states in male (high) female (medium) category in 1991 shifted to male (High) female (High) category in 1997. The classification similar to the gender-disparity has been used to analyse location bias in literacy level. The male literacy in rural areas in most of the states is medium barring the states of Himachal Pradesh and Kerala which have high male literacy rates in 1991.

In 1991, most of the states fall into the category of (medium / low) rural and (medium) urban female literacy rate except the states of Kerala, Assam, Himachal Pradesh, and Maharashtra. Seven of these states have medium female literacy in both rural and urban areas. Assam, Himachal Pradesh and Maharashtra have high urban but medium rural literacy rate for females. Kerala is the only state which has high urban as well as rural female literacy rate.

In rural areas, all the states except Assam and Kerala have female literacy rate below 40 percent whereas in urban areas all the states have male literacy rate above 40 percent. The only state which has more than 60 percent literacy among female apart from Kerala is Himachal Pradesh in urban areas.

Rural male literacy level in 12 states have been above 40 percent whereas the female literacy level is below 40 per cent in 14 states. Himachal Pradesh is the only exceptional state other than Kerala where literacy level exceeds 60 percent for rural male. The rural literacy rate in Assam is less than 60 percent where it is above 60 percent the urban.

In some of the states the variations among literacy rates of these two segments of population are negative i.e. the literacy rates for Schedule Castes in these states are more than the literacy rates for all population. Other striking feature of literacy variation is that the differences in literacy rates are much more in urban areas than in rural areas. But these variations are small among male and female population. The variations among literacy rates of Scheduled Tribes and all population are glaring in most of the states. The variations in case of Scheduled Tribes are high in rural areas whereas the variations among Scheduled Castes were high in urban areas. The Scheduled Tribe male literacy rate exhibits different pattern than the Scheduled Castes male literacy rates in rural areas.

Most of the states except Assam, Uttar Pradesh, Bihar and Himachal Pradesh have literacy variations more than 15 percent. female ST literacy rates in rural areas also have similar pattern. Eight states have literacy variations among rural females more than 15 percent. The growth pattern of states for rural literacy have same trend for all population and for Scheduled Castes but the scenario is different for Scheduled Tribes.

In rural areas, the male enrolment rate has high correlation with female enrolment rate meaning thereby that female enrolment is high wherever the male enrolment is high at this stage of education and vice-versa. The female enrolment rate also have significant correlation with the parameters. This indicates that the female enrolment rate is high in the states where proportion of students promoting from one stage to other is high i.e. the level of development of education is high.

In urban areas, however, the parameter 'Male Enrolment Rate' and 'Female Enrolment Rate' have high correlation among themselves and the parameters (iii) and (iv) also have very high correlation among themselves. The first PC extracted for urban areas has significant factor loadings for the variables (iii) and (iv) and thus can be named as 'Promotion from Primary to Upper Primary Stage of Education'. The Second PC extracted for urban areas have high factor loadings for parameters (I) and (ii) and thus can be named as the factor 'Enrolment Rate'. The states which are leading both in rural as well as urban areas are Kerala and Himachal Pradesh whereas the states of Punjab, Haryana, Uttar Pradesh are among the first five ranking states in urban areas and the states of Tamil Nadu, Maharashtra and Gujarat have high ranks for rural areas.

States which rank last in order of both in rural and urban areas are Assam, Andhra Pradesh and Rajasthan. Whereas the states lagging behind in rural areas only are Uttar Pradesh and Bihar and the States having last ranks only for urban areas are Gujarat and Madhya Pradesh. The states which have ranks for rural areas better than the urban ranks are Assam, Gujarat, Himachal Pradesh, Karnataka, Madhya Pradesh, Maharashtra, Orissa, Rajasthan and Tamil Nadu. Bihar and Rajasthan are the states classified as highly backward States for both rural and urban areas whereas the rural areas of Uttar Pradesh and Urban areas of West Bengal, Orissa, Andhra Pradesh, Gujarat, Madhya Pradesh and Assam have highly backward status. Rural areas of Tamil Nadu and Himachal Pradesh are highly developed whereas both the rural and urban areas of Kerala are highly developed.

The states which have high ranks in both rural and urban areas are Gujarat, Himachal Pradesh, Kerala, Tamil Nadu and

Maharashtra whereas Karnataka and Madhya Pradesh have higher ranks for urban areas only. The states which have last ranks both in rural and urban areas are Bihar, Rajasthan and Uttar Pradesh whereas Andhra Pradesh and Assam are lagging behind in rural areas and Tamil Nadu is lagging behind in Urban areas. The states having rural ranks better than urban ranks are Himachal Pradesh, Kerala and Orissa. The analysis reveals that in rural areas Andhra Pradesh and Bihar have low ranks for all the variables whereas Uttar Pradesh has this status for all the variables except the variable and Rajasthan has this status for all the variable on the other hand Andhra Pradesh, Rajasthan have low ranks for variable and Rajasthan and Haryana have low ranks for variable.

The states which have last ranks for both rural and urban areas are Andhra Pradesh, Bihar, Rajasthan and Uttar Pradesh whereas Madhya Pradesh is lagging behind in rural areas and West Bengal has not developed this variable in urban areas. The comparison of level of development of this parameter among states reveals that Uttar Pradesh and Bihar are highly backward both in rural as well as Urban areas.

The rural areas of Andhra Pradesh, Rajasthan, Madhya Pradesh are also highly backward in progress of education. Both the rural and urban areas of Kerala are highly developed whereas the urban areas of Tamil Nadu are highly developed in education and Upper primary level. Composite Variable Rank The states which have high ranks both for rural and urban areas are Kerala, Punjab, Himachal Pradesh and Tamil Nadu whereas Assam has high rank for rural areas only. The states which have low ranks both for rural and urban areas are Bihar, Rajasthan, Madhya Pradesh and Uttar Pradesh whereas Andhra Pradesh has low rank for rural areas and West Bengal has low rank for urban areas. The states which have rural rank better than the urban rank are Andhra Pradesh, Assam, Bihar,

Maharashtra and West Bengal.

In addition Andhra Pradesh has also been identified as backward state for rural areas by Principal Component method. The top ranking states for urban areas according to both the method are Kerala, Himachal Pradesh, Tamil Nadu and Maharashtra. In addition, Punjab has been identified by composite variable rank method as one of the five leading states. The last ranking states for urban areas identified by both the methods are Bihar, West Bengal, Uttar Pradesh and Andhra Pradesh.

West Bengal have low rank for most of the progress parameters followed by Rajasthan which is also lagging behind in female education. All these states have low composite variable ranks. The states of Himachal Pradesh, Maharashtra and Tamil Nadu have high male as well as female enrolment ratio and continuance rate. Kerala also has high ranks foremost of progress parameters. In addition, Composite Variable rank has identified Punjab as leading state.

In rural areas, Rajasthan is a highly backward state for all levels of education. Moreover, Bihar and Uttar Pradesh have highly backward status for primary and upper primary level of education. At upper primary level Andhra Pradesh and Madhya Pradesh also have this status. The highly developed states in rural areas are Kerala, Tamil Nadu and Himachal Pradesh. At upper primary level only Kerala has this status and at high/ higher secondary level Himachal Pradesh has highly developed status.

In India, particularly at school level, is characterised by poor quality of education. One of the dominant factor contributing to low learning apart from social, economic and numerous others, is the quality of teaching at the school stage. The schools at primary and middle level have very high teacher pupil ratios. There are evidences of one teacher schools also at the primary level. The scenario is much more disturbing in rural and remote areas. Lack of motivation and accountability are the predominant features among school teachers. The disparities in quality of teaching will be analyzed separately for rural and urban areas. In Andhra Pradesh there are wide variations in rural-urban status. It has backward status for rural areas but has highly developed status for urban areas.

In rural areas, although Kerala has first rank for all and composite variable rank is also first but it has Seventh rank for the variable 'Percentage of Trained Teachers'. In urban areas also Kerala has first Composite Variable rank but has first rank only for one variable i.e. 'Percentage of Schools with two or more Teachers'. Andhra Pradesh has high rank only for the variable 'Trained Teachers' both in rural as well as in urban areas. Tamil Nadu has maximum number of trained teachers both in rural and urban areas. Uttar Pradesh and West Bengal have high ranks for the variable 'Schools with two or more Teachers'. The prominent feature of the variable rank analysis among states is that in most of the cases either a variable is developed in both rural as well as urban areas or has not developed in either of the areas.

Haryana has third rank for rural areas whereas Gujarat is third in Urban areas. The states lagging behind in both rural and urban areas are Assam and Madhya Pradesh. Himachal Pradesh and Orissa have last ranks for rural areas and Rajasthan, Uttar Pradesh are among last five ranking states in urban areas.

The states for which rural ranks are better than the urban ranks are Bihar, Haryana, Kerala and Rajasthan. The states which have same rank for rural and urban areas are Andhra Pradesh, Assam, Karnataka, Madhya Pradesh and Tamil Nadu. Analysis of level of development in quality of teaching at Upper primary level of education reveals that Assam is highly backward state in both rural and urban areas.

Rajasthan and Madhya Pradesh developed these facilities better in rural areas than in urban areas. Kerala and Bihar also have better development in rural areas than urban areas. The states which have highly developed facilities in both rural as well as urban areas are Tamil Nadu, Karnataka, Gujarat, Maharashtra, Andhra Pradesh, Haryana and Punjab. Composite Variable Rank Table presents ranks of the States for quality of teaching at upper primary level.

Tamil Nadu also has high composite variable rank but has low rank for the variable 'Pupil Per Teacher'. The comparison of variable and composite variable rank shows that other states also have similar pattern. The States which have high rank for one variable do have low rank for other variables. A cross sectional analysis of variable ranks and composite variable rank has thus been done to identify weak/ strong areas of the States. The rank of Madhya Pradesh (Rural) and Rajasthan (Urban) are low for 'Trained Teachers' as well as for 'Female Teachers'.

In Punjab and Haryana the rank for quality of teaching drastically changed from high to low during the period 1993-97 in both rural as well as urban areas. The deterioration in standard of teaching in these states during this period is the matter of concern. On the other hand, the teaching standard has gone down marginally from high to medium in rural areas of Tamil Nadu, Himachal Pradesh, Maharashtra and urban areas of Tamil Nadu, Himachal Pradesh, Maharashtra and Andhra Pradesh. At high secondary level, the correlation coefficients are positive but less than for all variables in rural areas.

But in urban areas, the correlation coefficient among the

variables 'Trained Teacher' and 'Pupil Per Teacher' is high. In rural areas one PC has been extracted for the purpose of analysis which has 1.58 as Eigen value and explains 53 percent of variation among variables. The extracted PC has very high factor loadings for the variables 'Pupil Per Teacher' and 'Percentage of Trained Teachers'. The factor loading for the variable 'Percentage of Female Teachers' is not significant. In addition, Karnataka (rural) and Gujarat (urban) are among last five ranking states.

The states for which rural ranks are better than urban are Uttar Pradesh, Tamil Nadu, Madhya Pradesh, Himachal Pradesh, Gujarat and Bihar. Assam has highly backward status in quality of teaching at high secondary level for both rural and urban areas whereas Orissa has this status for rural areas only. Urban areas of Orissa are covered under developed category. Rural areas of Rajasthan are covered under backward category but urban areas are included under developed states.

The states which have highly developed status for both rural and urban areas include Kerala, Tamil Nadu, Haryana, Himachal Pradesh, West Bengal and Punjab. The States which have first five ranks for both rural and urban areas include Punjab, Kerala, Tamil Nadu, Haryana and Andhra Pradesh. Among these the rural ranks of the states Punjab and Haryana are higher than their urban ranks. Other states among first five ranks in rural areas are Assam and Gujarat and in urban areas are Himachal Pradesh and Maharashtra. The states ranked among last five in both rural and urban areas are Bihar, West Bengal and Uttar Pradesh.

However, Maharashtra and Madhya Pradesh are lagging behind in rural areas and Assam is lagging behind in urban areas. State to be noted in this analysis is Assam which is among first five states for rural areas and among last five states in urban areas. Maharashtra on the other hand is among first five in urban areas and among last five in rural areas. There are large number of states which have high composite variable rank as well as high variable ranks for quality of teaching at High Secondary Level. But some states have low variable and low state ranks for a particular variable which is the areas of concern.

Tamil Nadu, which otherwise have overall high rank, has low rank in the field of 'Pupil Per Teacher' in rural areas. Similarly, Gujarat also has low variable rank for 'Female Teachers' in urban areas. Only state which has low Composite Variable and low variable rank for 'Female Teachers' both in rural as well as urban areas is Bihar. To analyse growth in quality of teaching during the period 1993-97 among states, the state's growth ranks have been compared with the ranks of the states for the year 1993.

In the states which had strong base in 1993, there was not much scope for improvement, whereas the states where ranks for 1993 were not good had comparatively better scope for raising the quality of teaching during this period. Thus, to have a realistic view of the growth of quality of teaching among states, it is desirable to have the comparative analysis of the states ranks for the year 1993 and growth rank for the period 1993-97.

Some of the states whose ranks have declined from High to Medium are Gujarat, Kerala, Haryana and Himachal Pradesh. The ranks of Kerala has gone down for rural areas perhaps because there was not much scope for improvement in this state during this period as they have already achieved high ranks in 1993 itself. In rural areas, the sub-variable 'Pupil Teacher Ratio' has positive correlation with trained teachers but negative with female teachers. But in urban areas, the sub-variables do not have significant relationships among themselves.

The States leading both in rural and urban areas in quality of teaching at higher secondary level are Kerala, Tamil Nadu and Haryana. Other states among first five ranks in rural areas are Maharashtra, West Bengal and in urban areas are Punjab and Uttar Pradesh. The states which are lagging behind both in rural and urban areas are Orissa, Bihar, Andhra Pradesh and Assam. However, rural areas of Rajasthan and urban areas of Karnataka are among the last five ranks.

The states which have rural ranks better than urban ranks are Himachal Pradesh, Gujarat, Maharashtra, Karnataka, West Bengal and Assam. The variations among rural and urban ranks are significant in Punjab, Himachal Pradesh and West Bengal. Assam is highly backward state in quality of teaching both in rural and urban areas at higher secondary level of education. Also Orissa and Bihar have highly backward status for rural areas. The highly developed states in both rural and urban areas are Tamil Nadu, Kerala and Haryana. In addition, West Bengal has highly developed status for rural areas and Punjab, Uttar Pradesh and Maharashtra have highly developed status in urban areas.

The urban areas of Rajasthan and Karnataka are covered under developed category whereas the rural areas of these states are backward in quality of teaching. On the other hand,rural areas of West Bengal are highly developed whereas the urban areas are covered under developed category. The states which are leading both in rural and urban areas in quality of teaching according to composite variable rank are Kerala, Punjab, Haryana, Tamil Nadu. The rural areas of Assam, Gujarat and Urban areas of Orissa are also among the top five ranking states.

The states which are included among last five ranks for both rural and urban areas are Andhra Pradesh, Karnataka and Uttar Pradesh. The rural areas of Maharashtra and urban areas of Bihar are also lagging behind in quality of teaching. There are some states which have low composite variable as well as low rank for the variable 'Trained Teachers'.

Karnataka has this status for both rural and urban areas whereas Andhra Pradesh is lacking in rural areas and Bihar has this status for urban areas. The states which have low proportion of 'Female Teachers' both in rural and urban areas are Karnataka and Uttar Pradesh. The rural areas of Maharashtra and urban areas of Bihar also have low ranks for 'Female Teachers'. The states of Assam, Orissa and Rajasthan although have high composite variable rank but the ranks for rural areas of Assam and urban areas of Orissa are low for the variable 'Trained Teachers'.

Also both rural and urban areas of Rajasthan have low ranks for the variable 'Female Teachers'. Madhya Pradesh has first rank in growth index for quality of teaching followed by Maharashtra, Rajasthan, Tamil Nadu and Andhra Pradesh. Among these leading states, Madhya Pradesh has sixth rank for Female Teachers' and Maharashtra has tenth rank for 'Trained Teachers'.

Whereas rural areas of Andhra Pradesh and urban areas.of Bihar have this status. There is no state which had low rank in 1993 and also had low growth rate during this period. At higher secondary level, the states of Kerala, Punjab and Rajasthan have high rank in 1993 and 1997 for both rural and urban areas. The composite variable rank is based on ranks of each sub-variable for quality of teaching.

Infrastructural Facilities

There are glaring disparities in infrastructural facilities among states and more so in the rural and urban areas. The facilities are worse at primary level of education. An attempt, has thus been made in this chapter to study the status of infrastructural facilities at different levels of education in various states. The analyses of infrastructural facilities will help us to identify areas requiring urgent attention for upgrading the basic amenities in schools.

For rural areas, the principal component analysis has extracted two principal components. The first PC explains 62 percent variation and Second PC explains 17 percent variation among . The first PC has high factor loadings for the variables 'Drinking water' and 'Lavatory/Urinal' facilities. This principal component can be named as 'Facilities for Drinking water/ Lavatory'. The second PC has very high factor loading for the parameter 'Population having schools within 1 km'. Second PC represents this variable. The two PC's together thus provide excellent summary of variables for infrastructural facilities. The PC extracted for urban area has high factor loadings for 'Drinking water' and 'Lavatory/Urinal' facilities and thus can be termed as 'Facilities for Drinking water/Lavatory'.

In nine states, the rural ranks are better than the urban ranks implying that development in rural areas in these nine states is better in infrastructural facilities as compared to urban areas. The analysis of educational development index of the states reveals that Bihar is the only highly backward state in level of development in infrastructural facilities both in rural and urban areas and needs more attention.

In Madhya Pradesh, Assam, Karnataka and Andhra Pradesh however, the rural areas are severaly lacking in the infrastructural facilities. The infrastructural facilities are highly developed in rural areas of Kerala and urban areas of Maharashtra, Gujarat and Kerala. In urban areas, nine states are covered under developed category whereas in rural area only Punjab and Haryana have this status.

Similarly, eight states are covered under backward category for rural areas whereas only the urban areas of Karnataka, Assam and Orissa have this status. The states which have same status for both rural and urban areas are Orissa (Backward), Punjab, Haryana (Developed) and Kerala (Highly Developed). In all other states, the development in infrastructural facilities in rural areas is less than the development in urban areas.

According to the composite variable rank the states leading both in rural and urban areas are Punjab, Kerala, Tamil Nadu and Gujarat where as the states leading only in urban areas are Maharashtra and Uttar Pradesh. Haryana is leading in the rural areas. The States which are lagging behind both in rural as well as in urban areas are Assam and Orissa. Andhra Pradesh, Karnataka and Madhya Pradesh are lagging behind in rural areas and Karnataka, Himachal Pradesh and Bihar have less development in urban areas.

The States where rural ranks are better than urban ranks are Bihar, Haryana, Himachal Pradesh, Kerala, Orissa, Punjab and Rajasthan. The states of Rajasthan, Uttar Pradesh and Gujarat have high ranks for overall infrastructural facilities but lack in a particular area. Rajasthan has low rank for the variable 'Percentage of Population having schools within one km' in rural areas and Uttar Pradesh has low rank for this facility in urban areas.

Gujarat has low rank for the variable 'Lavatory Facilities' in rural areas. On the other hand, Bihar has high rank for the variable 'Percentage of Population having schools within one km' for both rural and urban areas. Andhra Pradesh also has high rank for this facility in rural areas. Karnataka has high rank for 'Percentage of Schools with facilities of one or more rooms' for rural areas.

The states of Kerala, West Bengal, Haryana and Tamil

Nadu are leading in the level of development in infrastructural facilities at Upper primary level both in rural as well as urban areas. On the other hand, Punjab is leading in rural areas whereas Rajasthan is leading in urban areas. The states which are lacking in these facilities both in rural and urban areas are Assam, Bihar and Karnataka. However, Andhra Pradesh and Himachal Pradesh are lacking these facilities in rural areas only and Maharashtra and Orissa is lacking the facilities in urban areas.

The facilities are highly developed in rural as well as urban areas of Kerala while in Punjab and West Bengal, the rural areas have developed these facilities. Kerala has first rank for almost all the variables in rural and urban areas. Punjab which has second Composite rank for rural areas has Seventh rank for the variables 'Population having school within 3 kms' and 'schools with one or more rooms' in these areas. Haryana, which has third composite rank for rural areas, has eighth rank for the variable 'Lavatory Facility' in these areas.

On the other hand, Assam which is last in composite rank has fourth rank for the variable 'Population having school within 3 kms'. Himachal Pradesh and Andhra Pradesh which are among last three states in composite rank in rural areas have higher ranks for availability of schools and rooms in these areas. While Punjab and West Bengal are leading in rural areas only and Andhra Pradesh, Gujarat and Rajasthan are on the top for Urban areas. The states which are trailing behind in both rural and urban areas are Assam and Bihar.

However, Andhra Pradesh, Himachal Pradesh and Uttar Pradesh, lack these facilities in rural areas and Karnataka, Orissa have not developed the facilities in urban areas. In Rajasthan, all infrastructural facilities have been developed in rural areas except for the availability of schools within the radius of 3 kms whereas in Andhra Pradesh schools in urban areas lack urinal facilities. On the other hand, the state which has not developed all the facilities but has made progress in one of the area is Assam which has high rank for availability.of schools within 3 kms.

Himachal Pradesh has better drinking water facilities in rural areas while Andhra Pradesh, Assam and Orissa have better ranks for the variable 'Percentage of Schools with one or more rooms'. Punjab, Kerala, Gujarat, and Haryana are leading in infrastructural facilities both in rural as well as in urban areas. Whereas West Bengal has better facilities in rural areas and Rajasthan have better facilities in urban areas. States lacking in these facilities both in rural and urban areas are Bihar, Assam, Uttar Pradesh, and Madhya Pradesh.

Karnataka lacks facilities in rural areas and Orissa in urban areas. States having rural ranks higher than the ranks for urban areas are West Bengal, Himachal Pradesh, Andhra Pradesh, Tamil Nadu, Orissa and Assam. On the other hand, both rural and urban areas of Kerala are highly developed whereas only rural areas of Punjab and Urban areas of Gujarat and Haryana are highly developed in terms of infrastructural facilities in the schools.

The states where rural ranks are better than the urban ranks are Assam, Andhra Pradesh and Punjab. Whereas the states of Karnataka and Uttar Pradesh are lagging behind in rural areas and Orissa and Tamil Nadu are last in ranking among urban areas. The states for which the rural ranks are higher than the urban ranks include Andhra Pradesh, Assam, Bihar, Orissa and Punjab.

In these states as compared to other states the development in rural areas took place comparatively at a faster pace. In urban areas, Haryana which has second composite variable rank has seventh rank for the variable 'Lavatory

Facilities'. Whereas Punjab which has third composite variable rank has seventh rank for the variable 'Urinal Facilities'. On the other hand, Orissa and Assam, Uttar Pradesh, Karnataka which have last composite variable ranks have high ranks for the variable 'Schools with one or more rooms'. Assam is the state which has low composite variable as well as low rank for almost all the variables both in rural and urban areas.

Bihar, Karnataka and Orissa lack lavatory / Water facilities in urban areas. In rural areas, these facilities are lacking in Andhra Pradesh, Bihar and Himachal Pradesh. Himachal Pradesh has developed drinking water facilities in rural areas. Andhra Pradesh has developed schools with one or more rooms in rural areas whereas Assam and Orissa has developed this facility for urban areas.

The leading states in development of infrastructural facilities according to both the methods are Punjab, Kerala, Gujarat, Haryana and Rajasthan for both rural and for urban areas. The states which are last in ranking for both rural and urban areas are Assam, Bihar, Madhya Pradesh, Uttar Pradesh, Orissa and Karnataka. All India rank for infrastructural facilities in rural areas is 11 whereas this rank for urban areas is 9.

The states leading in rural areas are Orissa, Karnataka, Assam, Madhya Pradesh and in urban areas are Himachal Pradesh, Gujarat, Rajasthan and Punjab. The development process is not simultaneous in rural and urban areas. The only state which is last in ranking in both rural and urban areas is Bihar. In rural areas the states of Maharashtra, Punjab, Himachal Pradesh and Rajasthan are lacking in availability of infrastructural facilities whereas in urban areas the states lagging behind are Madhya Pradesh, Assam, Karnataka and Orissa.

The important feature of the analysis is that the state of

Punjab is among first five states in urban areas whereas for rural areas the Punjab is among last five states. Orissa is highly backward state in infrastructural facilities for both rural and urban areas. The highly developed states for both rural and urban areas are Himachal Pradesh and Rajasthan.

Rural areas of Bihar has also developed these facilities. There are many states like Andhra Pradesh, Gujarat, Haryana, Kerala, Maharashtra, Punjab, Tamil Nadu, Uttar Pradesh and West Bengal which have developed these facilities in urban areas. The rural areas of Kerala and Assam and urban areas of Bihar are included among backward states for these facilities. Karnataka is a backward state for both rural and urban areas.

The states leading in Composite Variable rank in both rural and urban areas are Haryana and Gujarat. Whereas Bihar has high rank for infrastructural facilities in rural areas and Himachal Pradesh, Kerala, Rajasthan and Punjab have high ranks for urban areas. The states lacking in infrastructural facilities both in rural and urban areas are Karnataka, Orissa and Madhya Pradesh whereas the facilities are lacking in rural areas of Kerala and urban areas of Bihar. Punjab which has first composite variable rank for rural areas has fifth rank for first variable.

The next leading states, Rajasthan and Haryana have lower ranks for third variable. Bihar the next ranking state has lower rank for drinking water facilities. On the other hand, last ranking state Orissa for rural areas have third rank for facility for one or more room Karnataka and Kerala which are also last ranking states have high ranks for this variable. In urban areas, most of the states have similar status according to variable and composite variable rank barring few exceptions. In rural areas, Orissa has low rank for most of the variables whereas Kerala has low rank for development of facility.

Karnataka, Kerala and Orissa have developed the facility in rural areas whereas Karnataka acquired this status for urban areas. There are large number of states which have developed these facilities in both rural and urban areas. Gujarat has high composite variable as well as high rank for all the variable in rural and urban areas. Haryana and Rajasthan also have this status but for the variable 'Availability of one or more rooms' in urban areas.

Punjab also has this status except for the variables (iii) and (v) for urban areas. Other states having this status for rural areas are Bihar for parameter (I) and (ii) and Himachal Pradesh for parameter (v). The states leading in urban areas for most of variables include Himachal Pradesh, Karnataka, Uttar Pradesh. The states of Assam, Madhya Pradesh, Maharashtra, Orissa and Tamil Nadu having this status for variable (v) in urban areas. In rural areas, Assam has highly backward status for elementary education. Whereas Madhya Pradesh and Karnataka have this status for Primary as well as high secondary level of education while. at higher secondary level Orissa has been identified as highly backward state.

The other states which have this status for primary education are Andhra Pradesh and Bihar. In rural areas, Kerala has highly developed status for all levels of education except higher secondary level. Punjab has this status for upper primary and high secondary whereas West Bengal has this status for upper primary level only.

The states which have this status in rural areas are Bihar, Rajasthan and Himachal Pradesh. In urban areas, Bihar has highly backward status for elementary education. Assam has this status for upper primary and high secondary level and Orissa has this status for upper primary and higher secondary level.

Wherever, Karnataka has highly backward status for

upper primary and Madhya Pradesh for high secondary level. In urban areas, Kerala is highly developed state at all levels of education. Gujarat is also leading at all levels except upper.primary level of education. Maharashtra is leading in primary and higher secondary level and Haryana is leading at high/higher secondary levels of education.

At higher secondary level many other states like Andhra Pradesh, Himachal Pradesh, Punjab, Rajasthan, West Bengal, Uttar Pradesh and Tamil Nadu have high ranks. Development of education to a large extent depends on the availability of financial resources. Although, numerous research studies on educational expenditure have shown that there may not necessarily be a significant relationship between the growth of education and the financial resources available.

Educated people are likely to be more productive and hence better off. They are also likely to contribute more to a country's economic growth. At the same time, education reinforces the socio-economic dynamics of a society towards equality in attainments and opportunities for its people. Though, the returns to education may vary across individuals, regions, level and nature of education, in general, they are significantly higher for poor developing areas than for the rich. Education is therefore, the best social investment, given the synergies and the positivepeople in their well-being. It is also a priority for countries seeking to develop and sustain their level and pace of development.

The UNDP in its HDR 1990, pointed out, and rightly so, that literacy is a person's first step in learning and knowledge building and, therefore, literacy indicators were essential for any measurement of human development. There can be many indicators such as literacy rate for population as a whole or a part of the population, including, those for adults, females, the deprived and the backward. Other indicators like enrolment, attendance and dropout rates of the school going children or the girl child; or the proportion of population having higher and technical qualification, etc. could also be used to capture the level of educational attainment in a society. For instance, adult literacy rate (that has frequently been used as an indicator to reflect educational development in human development indices) may measure only a superficial capacity to read and write one's name or a simple sentence and, hence, may not be a good indicator in itself for capturing educational attainment of a society, particularly when it is a result of mass adult literacy programme and not an outcome of a formal education system.

Even in the case where adult literacy or, for that matter, literacy rate is a result of a formal education system, it is at best an indicator of stock of educational attainment for the society - reflecting the social effort for education over a number of years in the past - rather than a flow-variable, that captures the current spread of education. For a developing country like India, where literacy levels are comparatively low, where there are critical gaps in educational attainments across regions, population segments and, more importantly, there are significant returns to education - economic, social and political - to be reaped, it may be desirable to select educational indicators reflecting, for example, a social preference that lays greater value on acquiring literacy early on in an individual's life.

Among other considerations, this would enable an individual and society to benefit for a longer duration from cumulation of spill-over effects of his/her educational attainments. India's educational development is a mixed bag of remarkable successes and glaring gaps. In the post-independence period, the pace of educational development was unprecedented by any standards.

At the same time, perhaps, the policy focus and public intervention in the provisioning of educational services was not adequately focused or, even misplaced, to the extent that even after 50 years of planned effort in the sector, nearly one-third of the population or close to 300 million persons in age-group 7 years and above are illiterate. There are critical gaps in the availability of infrastructural facilities and qualitative aspects of education including, teachers training, educational curricula, equipments and training materials, particularly, in the publicly funded schooling system of the country. The attainments, as also the failures have not been uniform across all regions.

Though, the regional differences are indeed striking, there has been a significant reduction in inequalities in educational attainments across gender, population segments by castes, income levels and the rural-urban divide. The Census of India, currently defines the literacy rate as proportion of literates to total population in age group 7 years and above. It was merely 18.3 per cent in 1951, 43.6 per cent in 1981 and is 65.2 per cent as per the Census 2001.

In the decade 1991-2001 the number of illiterates declined, for the first time since the Census of 1951, by almost 32 million in absolute terms. There are, however, large inter-State variations in literacy rates in the country. At one end, proportion of literates was the highest in Kerala, at over 90 per cent, and at the other it was less than 50 per cent in Bihar for the year 2001. The regional variations in literacy rates have declined since 1981, though the disparities become more pronounced if one takes into account rural-urban differences or the differences between male and female literacy rates.

The literacy rate in rural areas increased from about 36 per cent in 1981 to 59 per cent in 2001. The corresponding rates in urban areas were about 67 and 80 per cent, respectively. Thus, rural-urban gap has declined from about 31 to 21 percentage points. During this period, literacy rate for males increased from about 56 per cent in 1981 to nearly 76 per cent in 2001. The corresponding change in female literacy rate has been from around 30 per cent to 54 per cent.

On the whole, the decline in gender gap, which peaked in 1981 at 26.6 percentage points, and was 21.7 percentage points in 2001, is less impressive than the decline in rural-urban gap. For rural areas, gender gap declined from 28 to 24 percentage points, whereas in case of urban areas the decline was a little higher at 7 percentage points. The inter-State variations in literacy rate for males were much lower in comparison to females.

Of the larger States, while Kerala is among the best performers in terms of literacy rate - both for males and females - Bihar continues to be at the bottom. The literacy rate for Scheduled Castes and Scheduled Tribes population has been much lower than the rest of the population. As against the overallliteracy rate of 52.2 per cent in 1991, the literacy rate for Scheduled Castes and Scheduled Tribes was 37.4 per cent and 29.6 per cent, respectively.

For others, the literacy rate was 57.7 per cent. Less than one-fourth of Scheduled Caste females and less than one female in every five among the Scheduled Tribes were literate. In case of Bihar less than 10 per cent of Scheduled Caste females and in case of Rajasthan less than 5 per cent of Scheduled Tribes females were literate in 1991. The situation was much worse in 1981, when only about 1 per cent of Scheduled Tribe females in Rajasthan were literate. The disparities in male and female literacy rate among Scheduled Castes and Scheduled Tribes were much higher than those for the rest of the population.

Notwithstanding the disparities in attainments on literacy across States, regions and population segments, there is a definite transition taking place in respect of literacy rates across

States in India. For instance, in 1991, there were number of States with literacy rate less than 50 per cent, but in 2001, it is only in case of Bihar that literacy rate is less than 50 per cent. The adult literacy rate, in India is defined as the proportion of literate population in age group 15 years and above.

Like literacy rate, adult literacy rate gives an indication of the stock of human capital in population. More particularly, it is a prevalence measure of education that reflects average social effort, in a society, over many years. Such a measure is relatively insensitive to current spread of education among children and underplays the importance of social investment in educating the young in a society. In addition, to the extent spread of adult education is significantly dependent on non-formal education system, adult literacy rate, in India, may not be a good indicator for capturing educational attainments of the population.

The proportion of adult literates in the population increased from about 41 per cent in 1981 to about 49 per cent in 1991. During this period, the increase in proportion of female adult literates was marginally more than that of males, thus, reducing gender disparity in adult literacy. The proportion of adult literates among females in urban areas of nearly 68 per cent was more than twice that of the ratio prevailing in rural areas. This difference in case of males was much less.

The urban adult literacy rate for males was 86 per cent, whereas in case of rural areas it was 64 per cent. For a number of States, adult literacy rate for females in rural areas was 25 per cent or less. Among the larger States that fall in this category, include Bihar, Madhya Pradesh, Uttar Pradesh and Rajasthan. Overall, the States of Andhra Pradesh, Bihar, Madhya Pradesh, Rajasthan and Uttar Pradesh had an adult literacy rate of less than 50 per cent in the first half of 1998. The enrolment of children in schools depicts the current flow or the spread of education. There are alternate measures that can be considered while analysing enrolment of children in schools.

Among the more commonly used measures, gross enrolment ratio, age-specific enrolment ratio, net enrolment ratio, dropout rates and school attendance rates, are relevant for capturing the flow aspect of the educational attainment of the population. Gross Enrolment Ratio refers to enrolment at a specified level of schooling, irrespective of the age of student enrolled, to the population of children in the age group expected to be at that level of schooling as per prevalent norms on school enrolments. Thus, for instance, gross enrolment ratio at primary school level, i.e. for classes I to V, would be the percentage of children in classes I to V to total number of children in age group 6 to 11 years. This ratio is indicative of the general level of participation at a given school level. It captures, to some extent, accessibility and capacity of the education system to enroll students.

The ratio, often, exceeds 100 per cent due to inclusion of over-age, under-age, as well as repeat students for the concerned class. The gross enrolment ratio in classes I-V was 94.9 per cent in 1999-2000 as per the Annual Report of the Ministry of Human Resource Development. In case of many States this ratio exceeded 100 per cent, more so in case of boys. For rural areas, it increased from 42.2 to 49.9 per cent while for urban areas the corresponding ratios were 69.7 and 72 per cent respectively.

The ratio for boys increased from 58 per cent in 1981 to 62.1 per cent in 1991. For girls, the ratio increased from 37.8 per cent in 1981 to 47.9 per cent in 1991. Thus, the rural-urban gap, as well as gender gap declined during the period 1981 to 1991. A break up of age group 6-14 years into 6-10 years and 11-14 years shows that age-specific enrolment ratio is significantly lower in age group 6-10 years than in age group

11-14 years in 1991, as well as in 1981.

Much of this difference in age-specific enrolment between the two age groups disappears, if one drops enrolment ratio of children at age 6 years, which is considerably lower vis-à-vis other age groups in both rural and urban areas. According to the All-India Educational Surveys conducted by the National Council of Educational Research and Training (NCERT) this ratio for age group 6-14 years was 63.2 per cent in 1993 as against 56 per cent in 1978. While the ratio increased marginally from 64.1 per cent in 1978 to 66.4 per cent in 1993 for age group 6 to below 11 years, the increase in age group 11 to 14 years was quite significant from 41.7 to 57.1 per cent, during this period.

There are, however, certain inconsistencies between the age-specific enrolment ratios derived from the Census and that reported in the Educational Surveys. A study based on survey conducted by the National Council for Applied Economic Research, reports enrolment rates according to income classes for rural areas. According to this survey, 67 per cent of children in age group 6-14 years were enrolled in schools.

The ratio was 60.6 per cent for those belonging to households with annual income less than Rs.20,000. It was 84.4 per cent for those with household income of over Rs.62,000. This gave an income gap of 1.39. The income gap is defined as ratio of enrolment rates in the highest to the lowest income categories. At the State level the survey shows not only lower enrolments in Bihar, Madhya Pradesh, Rajasthan and Uttar Pradesh across all income classes but a generally higher income gap in these States than in Kerala, Himachal Pradesh, Punjab, and Maharashtra.

Net Enrolment Ratio refers to proportion of the population, of a particular age group, enrolled at a specific level of schooling, to the total population in that age group. The ratio overcomes the shortcoming of both gross enrolment ratio and age-specific enrolment ratio, as it captures age-specific enrolment of students in the classes they ought to be as per the prevailing norms for school enrolments.

It is well known that students who start early or late, as per the prevalent school enrolment norms, constitute a large proportion of the total enrolment in schools in the developing countries. In some countries information on the actual age of a child, particularly in rural areas is also, often, not available or is inaccurate. In such circumstances the use of net enrolment ratio as an indicator for school enrolments may not be reliable.

Information on net enrolment ratio is available from two sources namely, the Sixth All-India Educational Survey with 30th September, 1993 as the date of reference and the 52nd Round of the NSSO for the year 1995-96. As per the Educational survey, net enrolment ratio for children in age group 6 to below 14 years was 57.5 per cent. In other words, of the children in age group 6 to below 14 years, 57.5 per cent were enrolled in classes I-VIII. The ratio was 64 per cent for boys and 50.4 per cent for girls. The income gap is defined as ratio of enrolment rates in the highest to the lowest income categories.

At the State level the survey shows not only lower enrolments in Bihar, Madhya Pradesh, Rajasthan and Uttar Pradesh across all income classes but a generally higher income gap in these States than in Kerala, Himachal Pradesh, Punjab, and Maharashtra. Net Enrolment Ratio refers to proportion of the population, of a particular age group, enrolled at a specific level of schooling, to the total population in that age group. The ratio overcomes the shortcoming of both gross enrolment ratio and age-specific enrolment ratio, as it captures age-specific enrolment of students in the classes they ought to be as per the prevailing norms for school enrolments.

It is well known that students who start early or late, as per the prevalent school enrolment norms, constitute a large proportion of the total enrolment in schools in the developing countries. In some countries information on the actual age of a child, particularly in rural areas is also, often, not available or is inaccurate. In such circumstances the use of net enrolment ratio as an indicator for school enrolments may not be reliable. However, at State level net enrolment ratio for boys in age group 6 to below 11 years in Kerala was seen to be lower than or close to that prevailing in a number of States like Assam, Bihar, Gujarat, Himachal Pradesh, Karnataka, Madhya Pradesh, Orissa and Tamil Nadu.

This is surprising, given the educational attainments in the State of Kerala. The NSSO data for 1995-96 gives a net enrolment ratio of 66 per cent forper cent of the dropouts. Similar, findings were reported in the 'PROBE' report. They found that of the boys who dropped out, 35 per cent did not want to continue and 47 per cent were withdrawn from schools by parents who cited factors such as schooling being too expensive, requirement of children in other activities and poor teaching standards as the main reasons for their decision. The corresponding proportions for girls were 16 and 66 per cent respectively.

With such a magnitude of drop out rates and, often, poor attendance rates in some schools as well, the use of school enrolment rates as indicators to capture the flow or spread of education in the country may not be accurate in capturing the current educational attainment of people. A child may be reported as enrolled in a certain class, but he/she may not attend school on a regular basis and in some cases when attending may be dropping out before the end of the year. It is only when the enrolled students are retained over successive classes that the indicator on enrolment becomes useful from the point of capturing the current educational progress of a society. In other words, intensity of formal education in 1978 for rural areas was about 73 per cent of urban areas rising marginally to about 77 per cent in 1993.

The adjusted intensity of formal education, at national level, was estimated at 2.04 years in 1978 and 2.70 years in 1993. For boys, it increased from 2.61 to 3.10 years and for girls, the increase was from 1.42 to 2.26 years. Between the two years, while gender gap declined from 1.19 to 0.84 years, rural-urban difference remained stagnant at 1.5 years. In 1978 it was 1.68 and 3.20 years for rural and urban areas, respectively and in 1993 the corresponding figures were 2.31 and 3.81 years. The unadjusted, as well as adjusted intensity of formal education vary significantly across States.

In 1993, among the major States, the former varied between 3.97 years for Bihar to 5.44 years for Kerala. However, the range for adjusted indicator increased from 1.69 years for Bihar to 3.94 years for Kerala and 4.3 years for Himachal Pradesh. This was on account of there being a larger proportion of children in age group 6-18 years not enrolled in schools in Bihar unlike in Kerala or Himachal Pradesh. In India, the responsibility of educational development and spread of literacy rests largely with State Governments.

The Central Government has also been taking initiatives, under its Constitutional obligations, to supplement the efforts of State Governments by meeting some critical gaps in public provisioning for literacy improvement, particularly in the educationally backward States. These efforts have taken the shape of an enabling policy framework - for instance, the National Education Policy 1986, and the more recent step of introducing the bill for making primary education compulsory in the Parliament, as well as specific programmes including the Total Literacy Campaign, District Primary Education

Programme (DPEP), Mahila Samakhya or the present initiative on Sarva Shiksha Abhiyan embodying some of these past programmes. In the nineties, there has been a visible improvement in educational attainment of people in some States.

It is encouraging to see States that were so far considered educationally backward making significant progress in their literacy levels. As per the Census 2001 Rajasthan, Madhya Pradesh and Andhra Pradesh followed by Orissa and Uttar Pradesh have made unprecedented improvements in raising their respective literacy rates. The increase in literacy rate of Rajasthan and Madhya Pradesh is by more than 20 percentage points in 2001 vis-à-vis 1991 as against an increase of 12 percentage points at the national level. The performance of these States along with that of Himachal Pradesh, Tamil Nadu, Punjab and some North Eastern States shows that no unique 'education model' explains the results in each of these States. There are, however, some elements common in the strategy for improving literacy level in most of these States. Improving accessibility of children, in school going age group, to schools and increasing enrolment rates have been backed in some cases by visible measures to improve qualitative aspect of schooling.

There were 5.7 primary schools per thousand school going children in age group 6-11 years in 1982-83 as against 5.04 schools in 1997-98. This marginal decline was some what made up by improved availability of middle schools from 2.44 schools per thousand children in 1982-83 to 2.75 schools in 1997-98. A number of primary schools may have been upgraded to middle schools during this period, partly accounting for the decline in availability of primary schools. For Madhya Pradesh, as well as Rajasthan the availability of middle schools, in particular, has shown significant improvement in the nineties.

A similar trend was noticeable in case of 'teacher-pupil ratio' - an indicator having a bearing on quality of education and, hence, on retention of enrolled children in schools. The ratio refers to number of students enrolled for every teacher appointed. This ratio has not changed significantly in the fifteen years between 1982-83 and 1997-98. During this period it increased from 40 to 42 students in primary classes, from 34 to 37 students in middle classes and remained same at 29 students per teacher for secondary classes. Thus, at the national level, the appointment of teachers kept pace with increasing enrolment in schools.

At State level, there are no clear trends backward States these ratios have either remained same or they have improved in the nineties except in case of Bihar and to some extent in West Bengal where there is a consistent and significant deterioration over the years. Public support by way of allocation of resources for creation and maintenance of education infrastructure has a direct bearing on some of these indicators. An important feature of the strategy in States that have made rapid strides in raising their literacy rates, apart from improved enrolment rates of children in school going age group, relates to the success school going age group, relates to the success in bringing down their drop out rates.

States like Rajasthan, Madhya Pradesh, Haryana, Tamil Nadu, Punjab and Maharashtra have been able to bring down their drop out rates significantly. In case of Andhra Pradesh, Bihar, West Bengal and Uttar Pradesh these rates have, however, stagnated. In some States, the involvement of Panchayati Raj Institutions in the management of local schools at primary and upper primary levels and schemes aimed at providing nutritional supplements in the schools, such as the mid-day meal scheme particularly in case of Tamil Nadu, have also contributed in improving enrolments and retention in schools.

Innovative changes in curriculum, including exposure to

vocational training; flexibility in scheduling of school terms, particularly in rural areas, keeping in view the requirement of large segment of children who are, invariably, drafted to meet seasonal demand for labour in agriculture sector; and evening/ night schools in urban areas have been seen to be helpful in improving enrolments and retaining children in schools for longer duration. An aspect of the current policy focus in education that has a bearing on the future prospects of educational attainment for the society at large relates to the education of the girl child.

Though, the Approach to the Tenth Plan aims at bringing down gender gap in literacy by 50 per cent over the plan period, the target seems ambitious, unless significant headway is made in States like Bihar, Uttar Pradesh, Rajasthan, Orissa and Haryana. Initiatives like the Mahila Samakhya that focus on creating a greater access to education, generate demand for education, build capacities and strengthen women's abilities to effectively participate in village level processes for educational development have to be pursued vigorously in these States having significant differential in male-female literacy rates. The level of employment, its composition and the growth in employment opportunities is a critical indicator of the process of development in any economy.

It is also an indicator that, in most cases, directly captures the economic attainments and hence the level of well-being individuals. In India, because of the nature of labour market, the data on employment is not entirely adequate or even reliable. The categorisation of the persons any category is determined on the basis of time-spent criterion. While the labour force participation rates are expectedly higher in rural areas in comparison to urban areas, in both cases there has been a decline during this period.

At the State level except for Haryana, Andhra Pradesh, Himachal Pradesh and the North Eastern States of Mizoram,

Meghalaya and Manipur, where a marginal increase between 1983 and 1993- 94 was followed by a declined subsequently, for all other States, there was a gradual decline in the labour force participation rates over the period 1983 1999-2000. These changes have to be seen in the context of the demographic transition in each of these States, as well as in terms of the proportions of persons delaying their entry into the work force for pursuing higher education.

The growth in employment for persons employed in the age group 15 years and above on the usual principal and subsidiary status has declined significantly in the nineties vis-à-vis the eighties. At the national level forthe period 1983 to 1993-94, the growth in employment was 2.1 per cent on the whole. It was 1.8 per cent in rural areas and 2.9 per cent in urban areas. In the subsequent period, the corresponding growth rates were 1.6 per cent on the whole and 1.3 and 2.4 respectively for rural and urban areas. The decline in the employment growth for females has been significantly higher than that for males.

In fact, in both rural and urban areas, it has declined nearly by half. At State level, Himachal Pradesh, Jammu & Kashmir, Rajasthan, West Bengal and Andhra Pradesh had an employment growth higher than the national average during the period 1983 to 1993-94. In the subsequent period, among the major States, only Punjab, Bihar and Assam have not only had growth rates higher than the national average but have also succeeded in significantly improving their performance over the previous period. Given the increase in the labour force, a decline in the growth of employment in the nineties vis-à-vis eighties has increased the incidence of unemployment.

The incidence of unemployment, defined as percentage of persons unemployed in the age group 15 years and above on the usual principal and subsidiary status to the total number of persons in the labour force, has increased at the national level from 2 per cent in 1983 to 2.3 per cent in 1999-2000. There was an increase in the incidence of unemployment both for males and females on the whole and in particular for rural areas. In case of urban areas, however, there was a sharp decline between 1983 and 1993-94 from 5.1 per cent to 4.6 per cent, which has been somewhat, eroded by a subsequent increase to 4.8 per cent in 1999-2000.

Among the major States, Kerala has the highest incidence of unemployment at nearly 8 per cent in each of the three years for which the data has been presented. In case of Haryana and Karnataka there is a secular decline in the incidence of unemployment during this period but for others there is no clear trend and in most cases, the incidence of unemployment is higher in 1999-2000 than in 1983.

In general, the share of elderly in the population is higher in the Southern States and relatively lower in the Eastern and North-Eastern region. It is also higher in Punjab, Haryana and Himachal Pradesh, which are relatively better off States. This is on expected lines as some of these States have done well on a number of socio-economic indicators and have also been successful in bringing down their population growth rates.

Surprisingly, the proportion of elderly to total population is also high in Orissa, which is among the poorest States in the country. The regional pattern is more or less similar for both rural and urban areas. Until a few decades ago, the issue of the elderly was not in the forefront of the development agenda in the country. High birth rates accompanied by high death rates kept the proportion of India's elderly at low levels.

At the same time, the traditional family structure including the prevalence of joint family system and the significant role of the elderly in decision making at household level ensured that most of the elderly in the society were looked after by the members of their respective families. Since the 1960s, the proportion of the elderly has increased due to a steady decline in mortality rates and consequent improvement in life expectancy, as well as due to decline in the fertility rates, which reinforces aging of the population. While technological advancements and improvement in health services is reducing death rate among the elderly, there is a considerable change in the physical and socio-economic circumstances of the older people with the transformation of traditional joint family system into nuclear families.

The gradual marginalisation of the elderly in the decision making process in an average family and the break down of the family as a traditional social unit that took care of the elderly, sick, widows and orphans has brought forth problems of the elderly in the society. It is also important to recognise thatwith the rising number of the old persons and their changing socio-economic and physical context, the proportion of the destitute among them may also, perhaps, be rising. Unfortunately, despite destitution being a critical social dimension of the problem of aging, the database on it is quite inadequate at present. The number of widows among the elderly is about three and a half times more than the number of widowers.

In most cases, the elderly have to depend on their limited savings or on support of their children and family members. There are some exceptions. The State of Kerala has demonstrated that the civil society institutions - charitable trusts and community health care foundations - the public health care system, andprivate medical practitioners collectively provide a reasonably effective, accessible and affordable medical health care system to people, both in rural and urban areas.

States like Himachal Pradesh shown that public health care system can deliver basic medical and health care services even in rural areas. The issue of shelter for the elderly, outside the traditional family system, the form of old age homes, community and recreational centres for the aged, have not addressed systematically both by public agencies as also the society initiatives in most of States.

In the coming years with increasing number of the elderly, more so of elderly women, makes it necessary to suitably reflect the economic, social and physical concerns of the older people in public policies, programmes and interventions as also in the mobilisation of the civil society. Education, in the context of such an approach, is a critical dimension of building an individual's capability and ultimately his/her well-being. And so is the need to have a healthy childhood that lays the foundation for living a normal expected life-span and a potentially productive life, none of which is eroded by working prematurely when physically the body is not ready, or because operations generate a fluctuating demand for labour that is seen to be best met by household hands, including the children.

Most of the children are pushed into work because of this nature of rural economy. In addition, there is always the consideration of augmenting family incomes. As per the 1991 Census, over 90 per cent of boys and girls among the working children in the rural areas were engaged in agriculture and related activities. While boys were equally likely to work in own cultivation and as agricultural workers, the proportion of girls working as agricultural workers was much higher. The employment structure of the urban child worker has been quite different and more diversified.

Only 20 per cent of urban boys and 30 per cent of urban girls were employed in agriculture. Around 35 per cent of urban boys and girls were engaged in household and non-household industries. Within this group boys were likely to work more in non-household industries vis-à-vis girls who worked mainly in household/domestic work. Much larger proportion of boys worked in trade and commerce than girls. With growing population, small or no agricultural holdings, mechanisation of agriculture operations and in general the limitation of agriculture sector to absorb the growing labour force productively, a large number of farm workers (who are unemployed or underemployed) are forced to migrate to cities.

The migration is more visible from the areas of dry land farming, when droughts and failure of crops reduce work opportunities on the farms. Most of these workers are engaged in low paid work in urban informal sector, particularly in construction and other unskilled activities. Given the unfamiliar environment and deprivation, children of these migrant families often end up in the work force as rag pickers and domestic helps. In the Indian Constitution, Article 45 of the Directive Principle of State Policy says: 'The State shall endeavour to provide, within a period of ten years from the commencement of this Constitution, free and compulsory education for all children until they complete the age of fourteen years'.

Ten years after the commencement of the Constitution i.e. in 1960, the State was nowhere near achieving the goal articulated in Article 45. In spite of the impressive progress made during the last decade or so, even now, this goal continues to elude the nation, notwithstanding judicial pronouncements in its favour. In India, right to education is a fundamental right. Every citizen is vested with the right to approach the Apex Court to get compliance with this right enforced, in case the State fails to provide the necessary infrastructure, facilities and services.

The main provision of this Amendment is to insert an Article 21-A in the Constitution of India which stipulates that "the State shall provide free and compulsory education to all children of the age of six to fourteen years in such a manner as the State may, by law, determine". Article 45 of the Constitution has been amended to read "the State shall endeavour to provide early childhood care and education for all children until they complete the age of six years".

Finally, a clause has been added to Article 51-A of the Constitution on Fundamental Duties stating that it shall be the duty of "a parent or guardian to provide opportunities for education to the child or as the case may be, ward between the age of six and fourteen years". The Government has clarified that even though the Constitutional Amendment makes it a Fundamental Duty of every parent/guardian to send his child/ward to school, there is no provision in it for punishment in case he or she is unable to do so.

The Government has indicated that it will try to facilitate the enforcement of this provision not through punishment but by the creation of new school facilities, filling up gaps and improving the quality of education. Moreover, the community will be entrusted with the task of enforcing the right to education and parents and other members of the community will be mobilised for this purpose.

Article 21-A makes it obligatory for the Government to enact a Central legislation to give effect to the Constitutional Amendment. At the time the Amendment Bill was passed, the Government promised that a Central legislation would be introduced spelling out the parameters of what is to be provided by the State for implementing the Amendment. The parameters will include teacher/pupil ratio, number of rooms, distance of travel from schools, quality of education etc. Moreover, the legislation will also create a mechanism by which a citizen who is aggrieved that the right to education has not been fulfilled, should be able to get relief at district and sub-district levels rather than filing Writ Petitions in the High Courts and the

Supreme Court.

This Central legislation was expected to be introduced and adopted by the Parliament at its monsoon session. Unfortunately the monsoon session has ended and the Bill is yet to be introduced. The Government had earlier set up an expert committee to calculate the financial implications of the Amendment. According to its calculation, the financial implication is expected to be Rs.9800 crores by way of additional resources every year or 0.5 % of GDP for 10 years which is the time frame envisaged by the Government. The increase in the provision for elementary education in the last budget has not been at all commensurate with this requirement of additional resources.

Sarva Shiksha Abhiyan

The Government has in the meantime launched a programme called Sarva Shiksha Abhiyan to ensure that every child is provided free elementary education. The abhiyan (campaign) aims at universal enrolment by the year 2003, universal 5 years of primary schooling by 2007, and 8 years of elementary schooling by 2010. The Sarve Shiksha Abhiyan is being implemented in a Mission mode. The National Mission is headed by the Prime Minister of India and includes representatives of political parties, NGOs, academicians, teachers etc.

Similarly, at the State level the State Missions are being headed by the State Chief Ministers. The SSA specifically targets the provision of quality education for all. It also provides for intensive teachers training and academic resource support in the form of Bloc Resource Centres and Cluster Resource Centres, Teachers Grants and School Grants.

The Government has calculated that under the SSA, the Government of India will spend about Rs.63000 crores over the next ten years. Another Rs.7000 crores is expected to be spent through the streamlining of various programmes. The State Governments will provide additional resources amounting to Rs.30, 000 crores as their share of the SSA. An amount of Rs.25000 crores is expected to come from the private sector and Rs.5000 crores from community sources.

The Public Report on Basic Education in India by the PROBE Team The PROBE Report, which came out in October 1998, is based on a detailed field survey carried out from September to December 1996, covering all elementary schooling facilities (defined as first eight years of schooling) in a sample of 1374 households in 234 randomly selected villages of Bihar, Madhya Pradesh, Rajasthan, Uttar Pradesh and Himachal Pradesh. These States account for 40 % of India's population, and more than half of all out-of-school children.

Role of Teachers

Most teachers at the primary stage have at least completed secondary schooling. About two-thirds received some pre-service training. Among the younger teachers, the level of general educational qualification is higher but the proportion of those who have received pre-service training is lower. Teachers' skills are vastly unutilised. There is little evidence of in-service training having a practical impact on classroom processes. Teachers feel trapped in a hostile work environment and lack of respect by the local community.

Most teachers convey a deep lack of commitment to the promotion of education in the local community. Some of them come with good initial motivations but they lose it over time.

The report says: "Indeed, among recently appointed teachers we often met people with genuine enthusiasm. The honeymoon, however, is short lived, as the morale of younger teachers is battered day after day". The main concerns of the teachers were: poor infrastructure facilities; parents' apathy towards their children's education; paralysing curriculum; unwanted postings; distracting non-teaching duties; excessive paper work; and unsupportive management. Apart from improving teaching environment, the other challenge is how to ensure teachers accountability.

One of the means for doing so is to get the village community interested in the schooling of the children. This raises the question of teacher-parent relations. The most common pattern was one of scant interaction between parents and teachers. The two formal institutions of such interaction are Parents-Teachers Associations (PTAs) and Village Education Committees (VECs). These institutions were quite dormant. Less than one-fifth of the schools surveyed had a PTA and even the PTAs that did exist met only once or twice a year for the sake of formality.

VECs were doing only a little better. By and large, they seemed to be token institutions with neither teachers nor parents expecting much from them. The panchayat supervision of local teachers may have some potential as an accountability mechanism. However, there seems to be a real danger of abuse by despotic sarpanchs. Thus lack of active parent-teacher interaction is a serious shortcoming of the schooling system as it exists today.

In considering measures for improvement, it is important to take a broad view of the potential tool of parent-teacher interaction. One should not rely only on formal institutions such as VECs and PTAs but should also look for outside channels of parents-teachers interaction. Parents, themselves illiterate in many cases, are powerless. Hence nothing improves. Lacking faith in the system, parents are half-hearted in their efforts to send their children to school. This further demotivates the teachers. Everyone's hopelessness feeds on every one else's. The children are the victims. The number of primary schools has tripled since Independence. Most rural households are now at a convenient distance from a primary school.

The cash cost of education plays a major role in discouraging poor families in sending children to schools, especially when the quality of schooling is low. North Indian parents spend about Rs.318 per year on an average to send a child to a government primary school. Assuming that they have a family of three children, this is a major financial burden. In a middle class family, sending young children to school on a regular basis is a relatively simple affair. In poor rural families, sending children to school is an exacting struggle. Contrary to the popular belief mainly engendered by the propaganda of the protectionist lobbies in developed countries, only a small minority of Indian children are full-time labourers.

The vast majority of them work as family labourers at home or in the fields, and not as wage labourers. There is a lot of merit in schemes for providing school meals. They promote school attendance by providing incentives not only to parents but also to the children. They improve the nutrition level of the children, and facilitate socialisation - sitting together and sharing a meal helps to erode the barriers of class and caste.

Even among poor families and disadvantaged communities, one finds parents who make great sacrifices to send some or all of their children to a private school. This is another source of evidence for their high motivation to educate their children. Private school teachers tend to belong to the privileged class, with an even lower proportion of women than in government schools. Their formal educational qualifications are similar to those of government teachers, but most of them are untrained.

Private school teachers also receive very low salaries - often one-fifth of the salary of a government teacher with similar teaching responsibilities. They often take advantage of the vulnerability of parents. They maintain an appearance of efficiency and discipline, but the teaching standard in many of these schools is no better than in government schools.

As country after India emerged from colonial bondage, governments of the newly independent States began the process of nation building through 'centrally managed guided democracies'. Ironically, the spread of education that this involved led to critical thinking on the centralised model and provided an impetus to more genuine democratic leanings. With growing democratisation, the spotlight began to play on sustainable development, environmental concerns, and quality of life issues. Governments, for their part, began to realise that the skills and talents of their people were their greatest resource, and that the role of education needed to be thought through afresh.

Development henceforth was to be 'of' the people, 'by' the people and 'for' the people. In such a scheme of things, education was to play a critical role - on this, there is a global consensus, demonstrated perhaps most strikingly by the assessment of the progress of nations in terms of the HDI or the Human Development Index, a measure based on the premise that development should give people a decent standard of living, allow them to lead long and healthy lives, and ensure that they are well educated. With the formal system catering only to the privileged few, 'continuing education' or 'lifelong learning' seeks to compensate by giving those who have missed the bus a second chance. Adult education in India has ancient antecedents - the country's rich oral tradition for the transmission of scriptural knowledge dates back several millennia.

People's Rural Education Movement

Community Aid Abroad has been supporting the People's Rural Education Movement (PREM) for the past ten years. PREM is a non-profit, secular, voluntary organisation based in the state of Orissa, India. It began its rural education programs in Mohana Block in Ganjam District in Orissa in 1980. It now works in four districts in South Orissa with over 600 villages. Its objectives are to eradicate poverty, illiteracy and economic disparity and to evolve value based social structures for ensuring the integral development of the people.

Its programs are comprehensive, focussing initially on rural education but increasingly focussing on broader issues of social justice as well as practical matters such as rural credit. PREM however particularly focuses on women in their work and have specific programs focussed with women. In 1989 PREM carried out a survey of 68 villages in Nuagada Block. The findings were sadly not surprising. Women are the most exploited of the community especially if they are from the poor and dispossessed tribal minorities.

Women make up over half of the population but contribute more than men, doing both work on the family land (usually held in the name of the man) as well as domestic work such as cooking, washing, looking after children, collecting water and firewood etc. They are paid less than men and have virtually no power. In the family girl children are unwelcome, uneducated, confined to the house and effectively enslaved until they die. Their position and lack of education leave them vulnerable to exploitation from husbands, landlords, money lenders, government officials etc.

In order to free women from these exploitative conditions PREM in its work in the area has established a women's program in which the following components are central:

- *the establishment of organisations for and by women at village, regional and block levels;*
- *separate training programs to create consciousness about women's problems and highlight these in public forums and media;*
- *women themselves taking up wider issues such as environmental protection, domestic violence, right of children, consumer awareness and community health; access to resources and training; credit; political representation.*

PREM's approach with the women's groups (mahila mandals) is very proactive. While existing mahila mandals may support women in their existing traditional roles, the groups PREM have started question the fundamental inequities in these roles and push for a much broader role for women in the community. This approach is not easy as there are a number of blockages to the process. There is a need to change fundamental attitudes in the community at all levels.

The most insidious are the lines that 'women are not prepared'; 'let us go slow'; 'slowly they will come up etc.' PREM believes the way to overcome this obstacle is to see that women have equal representation in all activities and that women are represented equally in village social and political institutions . PREM works to ensure that women have access to education and training and, therefore, to resources. PREM is training girls from grade one in all fields of life especially in the management of natural resources and human labour.

The method of training is with the catalysts approach

which not only trains people in technical matters but also looks to expanding the woman's conscious control and power in the community. The women's organisations also strive to establish new economic orders in their communities which recognise that child bearing and rearing roles are fully integrated and ensure the full protection of children's rights, especially those of girls.

PREM has promoted rural women to represent their villages in the panchayat and currently more than 30% of the seats in the panchayat (village council) are filled by women in the area in which PREM is working. NBJK, a people's organisation supported by PREM in the Mohana Block in Orissa nominated a woman to represent them as a chair person inthe Samity, the highest local body in the block. Another poor, illerate fisher woman was elected as one of the 11 councillors in the notified area council (cf municipal council) of Konark, a position never before occupied by poor fisher folk of the rgion, let alone by a woman!

Tribal women are under increasing threat from development which deprives tribal people of their land. The women are under particular pressure because their traditional roles involve collecting firewood and water, gathering minor forest products and producing edible cereals and pulses. Any destruction of the environment increases the hardship for women making them walk longer distances for gathering firewood and water for agricultural activities.

As a result PREM have realised that the best agent for ecological protection, preservation and promotion is the tribal women, because the environment is a matter of life and death. Any movement, whether economic, political, cultural, educational or ecological should be aimed at empowering the tribal women in these spheres. PREM has supported activities including bringing wasteland under green cover through planting fruit bearing trees, with intercrops like plantain, pineapple and locally grown pulses, cereals and oil seeds.

Part of this has included the building of watershed structures for holding all the rain and run-off water, thus preventing top soil erosion and increasing the ground water level of the area to improve drinking water availability. They have also trained people in sustainable agricultural practices to compensate for decline in land available for shifting cultivation. All waste land in the village is communally cultivated by women.

Women's Rural Savings Programme

The poor from the tribal, harijan and fisher communities in general are perpetually indebted to money lenders and landlords. As a result they remain dependent on these people in the economic, political and cultural fields. At present the usurious credit system leads the rural poor to increasing powerlessness. The modern banking system, though very efficient, is not accessible to the poor who have no assets or sustainable economic activities. As a result, no bank is prepared to lend them money particularly if they are women.

The 600 villages where PREM is active have been working on this problem and they have started their own method of fund raising and asset creation to meet their credit needs. This has involved the establishment of a sustainable and alternative credit system which can serve the interests of the poor. The system works by having both individual shares and group shares. Individual shares are Rs5-00/month while the groups shares are Rs25/month. These funds are deposited in the rural bank. The first two years of the program will consist of only savings with no credit being available.

During this time people will identify sustainable and viable income generation schemes for which credit may be needed. They receive training in this and after two years receive a loan. In this scheme the women's organisation will take the lead in the management and operation of the scheme.

Another innovative program of PREM's is the "100% literacy in 100 days". This is a literacy program as a genuine people's movement. The people planned and implemented the program with PREM offering guidance. The model of instruction for the program was "each one teach one". The aim is to reach 100% functional literacy in a specific period of 100 days. This means primary exposure to alphabets and numbers, the ability to read, to write the name and address and to make simple calculations.

A pilot project covered 300 villages. The campaign covered 22,000 illiterate people with 1,000 volunteers. The success of the campaign depends almost entirely on mass participation and to do this it needs mass mobilisation. Each volunteer had the task of teaching about ten families usually at home starting with the basics of writing one's name and address and moving on from there.

An external evaluation of the campaign found that 66% of the population could acquire the skill of reading and writing the name and address but more importantly half of the newly literate group were women. The 100 day functional literacy drive was followed by eleven months of people's education as a strategy for basic change in the attitude and lifestyle of the people.

Rishi Valley Rual Education Project

Rishi Valley Education Center is located in a chronic drought area, in the rural interior of South India. The population consists of marginal farmers and shepherds. The nearest city is Bangalore, about 120 miles away. The three main components of Rishi Valley Education Center are its Residential School, Conservation Program, and Rural Education Center, which cooperate on a network of activities in pursuit of main institutional goals of education and conservation work.

Rishi Valley School is widely regarded as one of the leading residential schools in India. Among its forty-five highly qualified staff members, some have taught in universities, twelve have PhD's, and most of the others have advanced degrees in their subjects. Students are chosen from a large pool of candidates, on the basis of character, talent and academic ability. Facilities for the staff and students are simple but well maintained.

The three-hundred acre grounds were barren when the school began. Decades of reforestation and water conservation efforts have restored abundant green cover all over the campus and beyond, and have regenerated one hundred and fifty acres of a once barren hillside behind the campus. With the help of private donations and government subsidies, solar panels and a biogas plant were installed to minimize our use of firewood.

Water conservation efforts, which include percolation tanks and small check dams, have succeeded in raising the water level in village wells for miles around. Nurseries raise nearly one hundred thousand saplings annually for free distribution to local villagers. A scheme is also underway to identify and cultivate traditional medicinal plants and train villagers in their use to treat common ailments.

Satellite schools participate in all these efforts directly and serve as resource centers for the transfer of knowledge and skills. These programs are changing our landscape and contributing to improved prospects for our disadvantaged neighbors. More than twenty years ago this unit was set up to provide free basic education, nutrition and health care for children from two or three local villages. Over the past eight years, under the guidance of two dynamic young co-directors, the Rural Education Center has been reaching out to a wider base of disadvantaged children: at first by establishing a network of "Satellite Schools" in villages scattered throughout the surrounding countryside, and then by evolving a comprehensive education program based on its experience within those schools. More recently a vocational training facility has been set up where young adults can acquire locally employable skills in typing, carpentry and tailoring. This facility was sponsored by a capital grant from ICICI (Industrial Credit and Investment Corporation of India).

Rural Education Programme

Rural educational program currently provides free education for more than seven hundred local village children within three concentric circles: a rural school on the campus, Satellite Schools in villages within a twelve kilometer radius of the campus, and some more distant auxiliary schools for which we provide assistance, materials and support, including preventive medical care. "Rishivanam", central rural facility, has been run as a day school campus for more than twenty years. It has become a model school, with one hundred children in vertically grouped classes up to standard VII and a rich program in crafts, music, athletics and puppetry in addition to its academic program. Many students continue their education through high school and beyond; some have returned to become teachers in the village schools.

Satellite School program began eight years ago with one school, "Valmikivanam," in a small off-road village several kilometers from the campus. The success of this experiment Ä which to some extent revitalized the whole village Ä persuaded the Education Secretary of the Central Government to support one or more new Satellite schools each year during the term of the grant. Sixteen schools have been constructed to date, and the target is twenty schools, the maximum number we can sustain and administer.

Each village provides land for its Satellite School, and the community gives whatever help it can in constructing a rustic building on the site, with one classroom and a storage space for teaching materials. The grounds are landscaped for water conservation and surrounded with trees to create an hospitable atmosphere for learning. Classes are "vertically grouped," with children of various ages and abilities sitting together to study one or several subjects individually or In co-operative learning groups.

Children learn from study cards which the teacher has made by hand as part of his or her training course; and the teacher guides them through the material. Satellite Schools serve as resource centers for their villages, for example by offering adult education classes at night. Literacy can spread throughout the village as adults and working children use the same facilities and materials for their own basic education.

Community participation extends to landscaping the school grounds and cultivating trees and plants that provide fuel, fodder, fruit and medicinal herbs for common use. This mixture of conservation and education taps into deep traditional associations between learning and forests, which benefit the whole village. To revive these ancient associations, each of the rural schools carries a Sanskrit name with the suffix "vanam", meaning "grove".

Teacher Training Program

Teacher training program began as a course for new teachers in the Satellite Schools. Local youth with minimal education learned how to handle children of mixed ages and varied abilities in a vertically grouped, one room school. During this course each teacher made a collection of study cards and educational games to equip the school where he or she would teach—materials which gradually evolved into the Education Kit. The Language component of the Education Kit was published in 1995, and is currently being used by a thousand schools in Andhra Pradesh. The Kit is currently being adapted in a dialect of Telugu for use in tribal schools.

Training program is currently active in three major areas: for independent NGO schools in Andhra Pradesh; for the Integrated Tribal Development Authority of Andhra Pradesh; and for newly established Government projects under DPEP and UNICEF in several other regions of India: Kerala, Tamil Nadu, Karnataka, Madhya Pradesh and Assam.

The education program that is comprehensive, economical, enjoyable and academically sound. This program is designed to address major problems in the Indian primary education system - whose schools have long suffered under the burden of poorly trained and demoralized teachers, inadequate textbooks, an oppressively high dropout rate and a chronic shortage of funds. Several years of experience with this program in actual classroom situations has demonstrated its potential for marked improvements in each of these problem areas.

The Kit has been designed for broad applications in the Indian context, including situations where qualified and experienced teachers are not available. It can be used by "barefoot teachers" as well as by more experienced educators. It can be used in formal as well as non formal schools. The text is up-to-date, focused on the local context and illustrated by local artists. Interwoven into the materials are values that nurture the sense of beauty, encourage tolerance for other cultures and promote regeneration of the environment. Attractive materials enhance student interest and raise the level of achievement.

A large collection of study cards is much more economical than individual textbooks. Each kit contains about 1500 laminated cards to be shared by many children. The cards are designed to withstand at least three years of hard use. With maximum sharing among students in a larger village, one Kit could serve as many as one hundred children at five different grade levels in three subjects for three years, reducing the cost of educational materials to as little as one fifth of the average cost of textbooks.

And there are additional long-run economies, because study cards can be replaced individually when they wear out;and revision or upgrading can be done at any time and very readily, card by card. The Kit is easy for teachers to use, because it renders each step of learning maximally concrete and facilitates a "hands on "approach for both students and teachers. This also makes for more efficient teacher training and lower training costs.

Evaluation procedures are provided to help teachers identify and remedy gaps in learning. This gives both student and teacher a sense of accomplishment to relieve the widespread sense of failure that has been demoralizing rural children. This Kit offers students a positive learning experience through attractive design and extended use of puppetry, mime and humor in the local idiom.

The Kit has been tested in practice with first-generation learners in fifteen "Satellite Schools", where students regularly clear the Grade Five state examination in four years. Also it has weathered rigorous external testing. Prototypes have been used in workshops conducted for educational administrators in both Government and NGO educational groups from all over Andhra Pradesh.

They have been examined by the Central Ministry for Human Resources, by the Secretary of Education for Andhra Pradesh, by Action Aid, UNICEF, and by officials of Central and State Councils for Educational Research. A recent evaluation conducted by the Education Department of the Andhra State Government demonstrated that novice teachers with three weeks of training were able to bring their students from zero to grade one level in six weeks, with an average success rate of 95% in one district.

By training local youth to work in schools located in or near their own villages, it is possible to secure teachers with a sense of commitment Ä often of dedication Ä who are accountable in turn to the community.

The first major project undertaken was a UNICEF sponsored program involving about 4000 children dropped out of grade I. With a 6-week training during summer about 95% of these children were able to go back to school and continue their studies at grade II level. The success of this program led to a collaboration with the Integrated Tribal Development Authority of Andhra Pradesh on improving about 1500 tribal schools.

This is a two year program involving preparation and production of materials appropriate to tribal areas, training resource persons and monitoring the program. The project is currently in progress. Under a District Primary Education Program (DPEP), with their help Kerala and Karnataka state governments have undertaken pilot projects (funded by the World Bank) to study the feasibility of adapting this methodology and materials transcreated in their respective languages.

The UN system supports a wide range of activities and programmes directly related to the elimination of child labour in India. Chief among these is the ILO International Programme on the Elimination of Child Labour (IPEC), which aims progressively to eliminate child labour through education, social mobilisation and awareness raising, legal enforcement and strengthening of institutional capacity.

A total of 121 agreements have so far been signed for implementing Action Programmes under IPEC in India. In addition to IPEC, ILO has implemented the Child labour Action Support Project (CLASP) aimed at enhancing the central government's planning and implementation capacity with regard to child labour. It will also be able to support ongoing and further projects by state governments and NGOs under the National Child Labour Projects. UNICEF has also played an important role in the elimination of child labour in India by supporting government and NGO activities in the area.

The primary focus of UNICEF has been preventing child labour through primary education. It has provided financial and technical support for legal enforcement studies along with workshops and discussions on child labour at the national and state levels. More recently UNICEF has been involved in combating child prostitution and trafficking by organising regional workshops. It is working with the National Human Rights Commission to co-ordinate policy and do advocacy work.

Many other UN agency-supported programmes are increasingly concerned with this problem. These include among others the UNDCP Programme for Street Children; UNESCO's Learning Without Frontiers (LWF) Programme; UNFPA's support activities in the contest of the Government of India's

Adult Literacy programme; UNIFEM's entrprenuership development programmes for women; UNAIDS' activities on child trafficking; and UNDP's South Asia Poverty Alleviation Programme.

UNDP with NORAD assistance, is supporting two major social mobilisation initiatives for getting children out of work and into school, one with the M. Venkatarangaiya Foundation in Rangareddy District of Andhra Pradesh and the other with the Centre for Rural Education and Development Action (CREDA) in Mirzapur District of Uttar Pradesh. Child labour elimination - forms a major area of assistance under the GOI-UNDP supported Community based Pro-Poor Initiative Programme (CBPPI).

There are also several joint initiatives within the UN system in India focussing on this area. The most important being the Joint UN system Support for Community Based Primary Education. This includes UNICEF, UNDP, ILO, UNESCO and UNFPA which aims at supporting government efforts on universal elementary education and making primary education more accessible and effective. It especially concentrates on disadvantaged and marginalised children, including child workers.

Other relevant joint UN initiatives include the UNICEF-ILO protocol regarding regular consultation and co-ordination on various aspects of child labour, the ILO and UNESCO Joint Convention On The Status Of Teachers, collaboration between UNICEF and UNAIDS on the prevention of child trafficking along with UNAIDS, UNICEF, UNESCO and WHO working together on HIV/AIDS prevention.

Over the past 50 years, there has been a significant growth in the number of new universities and institutions of higher learning in specialised areas. There are now 273 universities/deemed to be universities (including 18 medical universities and 40 agricultural universities) and 12,300 colleges (of which 4,683 are in the rural areas). The Ninth Plan reiterates the objectives/ policy directions of the National Policy for Education, 1986, and its Programme of Action, 1992.

During the Ninth Plan, an outlay of Rs. 2,520.06 crore was allocated for the university and higher education sub-sector against which an expenditure of Rs. 2,270.92 crore was incurred. The Ninth Plan period saw the emergence of separate universities for science and technology and health sciences, autonomous colleges with the freedom to design curricula, evolve new methods of teaching and research, frame admission rules and conduct examinations as well as Centres of Excellence and the National Assessment & Accreditation Council (NAAC).

There are also institutions of higher learning recognised as deemed to be universities with their own sources of funding in addition to Government grants. The major emphasis in strategies relating to higher education during this period has been on an integrated approach, with an emphasis on excellence and equity, relevance, promotion of value education, and strengthening the management systems.

Autonomous centres have been set up within the university system to provide common facilities, services and programmes to universities and for the promotion of quality. It is increasingly recognised that in the context of major economic and technological changes, the system of higher education should equip students with adequate skills to enable their full participation in the emerging social, economic and cultural environment.

Universities are thus witnessing a sea change in their outlook and perspective. Also, information and communication technologies are leading to fundamental changes in the structure, management and mode of delivery of the entire educational system. Many universities have already recognised the strategic significance of open and distance learning and offer correspondence courses. At the beginning of the decade, there were 64 universities offering courses through correspondence.

The developments in the field of information communication technology and expansion of infrastructure for communication all over the country have created an unprecedented opportunity to serve the needs of continuing education and also to meet the demands for equal opportunity for higher education. The basic issue of quality improvement would be addressed through the modernisation of syllabi, increased research, networking of universities and departments and increased allocation of funds.

Networking through local area network (LAN), wide area network (WAN), Information and Library Network (INFLIBNET) would also lead to increased academic activities and research. The university system would be expected to utilise the autonomy it enjoys for innovations in teaching and for pursuing high quality research. The emphasis would be on conferring autonomous status on more colleges, provision of the means to interact across geographical boundaries of institutions, improving the infrastructure, more rationalised funding of research, integration of teaching, research and evaluation, and mutual collaboration and cooperation among universities for optimum utilisation of available resources.

There is a pressing need to improve the management and governance of universities to better enforce financial and administrative discipline. Decentralisation of the university system, greater powers to faculty/ departments and nomination of students to university bodies on the basis of merit/excellence are, therefore, issues which would receive attention. The accreditation process should be made more transparent, time-bound and be progressively freed of Government regulations and control leading to a situation when the whole procedure would be based on a system of public appraisal/acceptance. Financing of higher education is another critical issue. The fee structure in the universities is abysmally low and has remained static for more than three decades.

The universities should, therefore, make efforts to rationalise the fees and attempt greater generation of internal resources. The extent to which universities can hike fees needs to be studied, including avenues for receipt of contributions, donations, gifts, and sponsorships from the alumni, trusts, private sector and industries. However, utmost care needs to be taken to ensure that the social obligation - ensuring that the poorer students are given adequate opportunity to pursue higher education - is not lost sight of.

University Grants Commission (UGC). The UGC, the apex body responsible for the development of higher education in the country, has been providing financial assistance to all eligible central, state and deemed universities, both under Plan and non-Plan heads, for improving infrastructure and basic facilities. The grants-in-aid would be used for setting up central universities especially in states that do not have one, more autonomous colleges and providing support to private colleges.

Attempt would be made to ensure that the socially, economically and geographically disadvantaged sections are able to access higher education. To encourage more women to pursue higher studies, the number of counselling/study centres, day care centres for children and hostels will be increased during the Tenth Plan. Similar steps will be taken for scheduled caste/scheduled tribes (SCs/STs) students and minorities.

Besides, the activities of distance/open universities will be supported to increase access for the northeastern and backward areas. The UGC proposes to promote quality and relevance in higher education in the Tenth Plan by initiating complementary skill-oriented courses. The career development of students will be promoted through courses with a professional focus.

A major programme of vocationalisation of education has already been initiated in 35 subjects at the undergraduate level. In the Tenth Plan, new courses, including vocational courses, relating emerging areas such as information technology, biotechnology, biomedicine, genetic engineering, applied psychology, tourism and travel, physical education and sports would be introduced in more and more universities. The UGC has been continuously updating curriculum and the process has been completed in 30 subjects in different disciplines. The Administrative Staff Colleges (ASCs) have proved to be good instruments for teacher training and orientation.

Efforts will be made to widen and enhance the range and scope of ASCs and set up more ASCs to achieve a uniform regional spread. Steps have been taken from time to time for making accreditation of institutions mandatory. State Governments would be required to play a pro-active role in the accreditation process and help NAAC in its efforts to sensitise the stakeholders. (NET) to ensure minimum standards for those joining the teaching profession and taking up research in humanities including languages, social sciences, computer applications and electronic sciences. The Government and the UGC will continue to support NET and increase the number of research fellowships.

Universities and colleges are to be provided with Intranet and Internet connectivity to develop an IT orientation in higher education and will also be encouraged to set up LAN and WAN so as to enable connectivity within the campus and among colleges/universities. Under the ongoing scheme of strengthening scientific research, the UGC would continue to assist university departments, which have achieved excellence in research in different disciplines of science, especially in the emerging areas of biotechnology, biomedicine, genetic engineering, nuclear medicine, social science, humanities etc.

In view of the resource crunch faced by the UGC and the higher education system, it is proposed to give incentives to universities/colleges, which make efforts to increase/raise internal resources. The non-formal system (distance and open learning) accounts for only a 13 per cent of the total enrolment in higher education. Out of 7.7 million students enrolled in university and colleges, the distance education/correspondence courses covered only one million students.

The distance and open learning system provides flexibility in terms of combination of courses, age of entry, pace of learning and methods of evaluation. The coverage of open universities would, therefore, need to be extended to the backward regions, remote inaccessible tribal areas of the northeast and some of the eastern states. At present, there are nine state open universities and 64 Institutes of Correspondence Courses and Directorates of Distance Education in conventional universities.

The enrolment of distance learners in open and distance education System is expected to rise significantly in the Tenth Plan period. IGNOU has expanded its regional centres and network of study centres in the Ninth Plan period. It now has 46 regional centres and 691 study centres. It has been vested with the twin responsibilities of acting as an Open University and offering need-based education, training and extension programmes, with special focus on the disadvantaged sections of the society and acting as the national nodal agency to determine and maintain standards in distance education.

Education Council (DEC) to act as the nodal agency for distance education system at the tertiary level.

The university has adopted an integrated multimedia instructions strategy consisting of print material and audio-video programmes, supported by counselling sessions at study centres. It manages a dedicated 24-hour satellite TV channel, Gyan Darshan, which beams educational programmes from school to tertiary level 24 hours a day. Preparations are on to launch 40 FM educational radio channels (known as Gyan Vani) under a Memorandum of Understanding with Prasar Bharati. During the Tenth Plan, IGNOU would set up open universities in states where none exist at present expand the activities of Gyan Darshan and Gyan Vani.

The target is to extend the coverage of the open learning system to the backward regions, remote inaccessible areas of the northeast and low female literacy blocks in some of the eastern states. The Government, in April 2002, constituted the Committee on Promotion of Indian Education Abroad (COPIEA) under the chairmanship of Secretary, Department of Secondary & Higher Education. With the globalisation of the Indian economy, student mobility across national boundaries has increased phenomenally in the higher, technical and management sectors. A large number of foreign educational institutes have also started establishing their presence in India and there is immense potential for Indian educational institutions to set up campuses abroad.

The COPIEA will monitor all activities aimed at promoting Indian education abroad and will regulate the operation of foreign educational institutions to safeguard the interests of the students and the larger national interest as well. To this end, a system of registration will be introduced under which institutions will have to furnish information on operations and adhere to certain guidelines relating to publicity, maintenance of standards, charging of fees, granting of degrees etc.

The COPIEA would, over a period of time, develop a sectoral policy on foreign direct investment in the education sector. The higher education system includes research institutions that are outside the university system. These are the Indian Council of Social Science Research (ICSSR), Indian Council of Philosophical Research (ICPR), Indian Council of Historical Research (ICHR), and Indian Institute for Advanced Studies (IIAS) and the National Council of Rural Institutes (NCRI).

As these institutes have been doing valueable research on current political, social and economic issues, which are of great relevance, the Tenth Plan would be increase funding for them. They would also be subjected to external evaluations, including peer review, to increase their effectiveness. The technical and management education sector has made immense contribution to the country's economic and industrial development. It has produced high quality skilled, technical and managerial manpower.

Technical / management education is provided through the Indian Institutes of Technology (IITs), Indian Institutes of Management (IIMs) and 17 Regional Engineering Colleges (RECs). Other institutions in the central sector are: Indian Institute of Science (IISc), Bangalore, Indian Institute of Information Technology and Management (IITM), Gwalior, Indian Institute of Information Technology (IIIT), Allahabad, Indian School of Mines (ISM), Dhanbad, School of Planning and Architecture (SPA), New Delhi, National Institute of Foundry and Forge Technology (NIFFT), Ranchi, National Institute of Training and Industrial Engineering (NITIE), Mumbai, Technical Teachers' Training Institutes (TTTIs), North Eastern Regional Institute of Science and Technology (NERIST) and Sant Longowal Institute of Engineering and

Technology (SLIET). The number of institutes has grown phenomenally.

In 1947, there were only 46 engineering colleges and 53 polytechnics with an annual intake of 6,240 students. Due to initiatives taken during successive Plan periods, and particularly because of large-scale private sector participation, the number of All India Council of Technical Education (AICTE)- approved technical and management institutions has risen to 4,791 in 2001-02 with an annual intake of 6.7 million students.

The Ninth Plan period saw a phenomenal increase in the number of institutions in the technical and management education sector in the country with the AICTE granting approval for the setting up of 1,715 institutions across the country mainly through private initiatives. These cover courses/ programmes in engineering, technology, management, architecture, town planning, pharmacy, applied arts and crafts etc. There has also been a corresponding increase in the enrolment of students to meet the growing demand for quality technical/ managerial manpower, especially in the field of information technology (IT) and IT related fields.

Networking facilities have also been upgraded. There is greater use of technology in the teaching-learning process in the IITs in transforming pedagogy etc. The community polytechnics scheme started in 1978-79 made substantial contributions towards transfer of advanced technologies at low cost to the rural population and cost-effective strategies to upgrade skills. A large number of central, state and accredited technical institutions in the private sector have benefited under the schemes of Modernisation and Removal of Obsolescence, Research and Development, initiated in the Seventh Plan and Thrust Areas in Technical Education started in the Ninth Plan.

Infrastructure facilities for research and development

(R&D) have been upgraded under these schemes. Special emphasis has been given to strengthening the infrastructure facilities in the premier institutes viz., IITs, IIMs, IISc, RECs, etc. Besides, the IITs and IISc have implemented Technology Development Missions in the areas of food processing engineering, material technology, genetic engineering, biotechnology etc. The Technology Development Missions, started in the Eighth Plan, succeeded in establishing strong industry-institute linkages.

Technologies developed in projects carried out under different programmes have been successfully transferred to industry. Technician Education has been strengthened and the quality of students passing out of Polytechnics has improved through the World Bank-assisted state sector project which covered 279 polytechnics in nine states in the first phase and 249 polytechnics in ten states in the second phase. A National Programme of Human Resource Development (HRD) in IT targeting mainly IT education at the degree level and beyond, was launched in January 2000 in pursuance of the recommendations made by the Task Force on HRD in IT.

The components of this programme, include upgrading of computing facilities and connectivity; promotion of technology-enhanced IT education; faculty development initiatives; curriculum and course initiatives; and promotion of interface with industry. Further, a Task Force constituted by the Planning Commission to suggest strategies for India's transformation into a knowledge superpower, has highlighted how advances in IT, biotechnology and other emerging areas could be harnessed for India's economic and social development.

5

Challenges of Education for All

The Dakar Framework for Action based on national EFA assessments which highlighted that: 113 million primary school-aged children - mostly girls are out of school; there are 880 million illiterate adults in the world - most of whom are women; educational quality is often unacceptable; and that poverty, child labour, violence and conflict, and HIV/AIDS all have an increasing impact on education.

A number of goals were set in order to meet these challenges, each with special relevance to Education for rural development. The first goal is the expansion and improvement of comprehensive early childhood care and education especially for the most vulnerable and disadvantaged. This requires a special focus on expansion in underserved rural areas where the needs for childcare and preschool education are often greatest.

Continuing on, the Framework calls for ensuring that, by 2015, all children, with a special emphasis on girls and children in difficult circumstances, have access to and complete free and compulsory primary education of good quality. This goal compels governments to educate all children, even the most difficult to reach, living in remote and rural areas.

Therefore, there is a need to seek them out and find ways to keep them in school or in alternative, but equivalent, programmes. Furthermore, the Framework aims to ensure that the learning needs of all young people and adults are met through equitable access to appropriate learning and life skills programmes.

This requires that such programmes are appropriate also to the learning and working needs of youth and adults in rural areas. Another target has been set for a 50 per cent improvement in levels of adult literacy adult literacy adult literacy adult literacy adult literacy by 2015, especially for women, and equitable access to basic and continuing education for all adults.

The implication here is the need for special efforts in rural areas where most illiterates (especially women) live. Additional goals of the Framework include the elimination of gender quality in education by 2015, with a focus on ensuring girls' full and equal access to and achievement in basic education of good quality. This requires immediate and urgent attention to the 2005 goal and longer-term focus on the special problems of achieving gender equality in rural areas.

Finally, the Framework calls for the improvement of all aspects of the quality of education quality of education quality of education quality of education quality of education, so that recognized and measurable learning outcomes, especially in literacy, numeracy, and essential life skills, are achieved by all. This goal specifically addresses the disparities in quality between rural and urban areas.

The Dakar World Education Forum highlighted several strategies aimed at meeting the goals and objectives for education for rural development. They include:

— *promoting EFA policies within a sustainable and well-integrated sector framework clearly linked to poverty elimination and development strategies;*

— *ensuring the engagement and participation of civil society in the formulation, implementation, and monitoring of strategies for educational development and the development of responsive, participatory, and accountable systems of educational governance and management;*

— *meeting the educational needs of those affected by conflict, natural disasters and instability;*

— *conducting educational programmes in ways that promote mutual understanding, peace and tolerance and help to prevent violence;*

— *implementing integrated strategies for gender equality in education recognising the needs for changes in attitudes, values, and practices;*

— *urgently implementing education programmes and actions to combat HIV/AIDS;*

— *using new information and communication technologies to achieve EFA goals; and*

— *creating safe, healthy, inclusive, and*

— *equitably resourced educational environments.*

This includes the provision of adequate water and sanitation facilities; access to, or linkages with, health and nutrition services; policies and codes of conduct which enhance physical, psycho- social and emotional health of teachers and learners; and education content and practices leading to knowledge, attitudes, values, and life skills needed for self-esteem, good health, and personal safety.

The Dakar Framework for Action does not deal

specifically with Education for Rural Development (ERD), although it does say that "a key challenge is to ensure that the broad vision of Education for All (EFA) as an inclusive concept is reflected in national government and funding agency policies... Using both formal and non-formal approaches, it must take account of the needs of the poor and the most disadvantaged, including working children, remote rural dwellers and nomads, and ethnic and linguistic minorities, children, young people and adults affected by conflict, HIV/AIDS, hunger and poor health; and those with special learning needs."

In order to strengthen the ERD components in EFA plans, it is necessary to build awareness and capacity of MOE staff around a concern for ERD in EFA planning and implementation, by asking questions such as: Why do it? What is it? And how can it be implemented? Furthermore, it is necessary to analyze education contexts and needs of rural people better in order to clarify the most critical issues and components to be addressed in EFA plans, guidelines or checklists.

Finally, ERD components in EFA plans can be strengthened through the exchange of best practices on how to provide quality education to those most excluded and difficult to reach, in a cost-effective manner, and by enlisting ministries of agriculture to help ministries of education achieve their EFA goals.

Policies on Rural Schools

In US, the majority of states with acreage guidelines follow recommendations made in 1953 by the Council of Educational Facility Planners, International (CEFPI). They suggest a minimum of 10 acres for elementary schools, 20 acres for middle schools and 30 acres for high schools, plus one additional acre per 100 students. There are many policy variations among states, which also complicates matters.

Some states differentiate between existing schools and new construction. Alabama, for example, lowers the acreage requirements for additions or renovations to existing schools. And in several states, the per-pupil acreage required for small schools is higher than that for large schools. In almost all states, the school facility policies allow for exemptions or alternatives to state-required acreage.

In South Carolina, for example, schools constructed within the past 30 years consume 33 percent more land per pupil than older facilities. And similarly, in North Carolina, schools built in the past 15 years are located on sites that average over 70 acres, while older schools have a median site size of 27 acres. Thus, the belief that "bigger is better" for school enrollment is also applied to school site requirements. This trend puts pressure on existing small rural schools that want and need to renovate or expand.

Though almost 69 percent of schools in the United States have been closed since 1940, many rural communities are still served by small schools. These schools are fre-quently located within small towns or villages-places where meeting requirements for excessive acreage is difficult or impossible. Acreage policies actually create incentives to close and consolidate rural and small schools: either these schools find a way to provide more land or they risk losing state aid or state approval for a needed facility project.

Some of this pressure on small schools is the result of acreage formulas themselves. Most acreage formulas place a higher burden per pupil on smaller schools than on larger schools. Using the old CEFPI guidelines, for example, a middle school of 200 students would have to find a site of 22 acres, or

.11 acres per student. A middle school serving 600 students, however, would only have to provide a site of 26 acres, or .043 acres per student. A high school serving 200 students would have to offer 32 acres, or .16 acres per student, while a high school serving 2,000 students would only be required to provide a site of 50 acres, or .025 acres per student.

To meet acreage requirements, schools must often be moved out of existing population centers and farther away from the communities they serve. This disloca-tion can weaken ties between the local community and schools. It also can make it more difficult for parents to remain engaged with their children's schools. For students, relocating away from population centers results in longer bus rides and all the problems associated with this. None of these consequences are positive, and all threaten to dismantle some of the recognized benefits of rural schooling.

In addition, removing local schools from small towns and villages weakens them economically. Closing schools can erode the tax base, deplete remain-ing schools of resources, and reduce property values in areas where they were located. Studies indicate that closing a local school in a small town often means losing both a major employer with a significant annual budget and payroll and the income from purchases by the school and its employees.

In addition, when a school closes, the value of local property declines, hastening the exodus of young families from the area and limiting its ability to attract newcomers. Acreage policies that dictate the size of school sites diminish local control over the size and location of schools that serve these communities Some rural communities may wish to build a new school on a larger site. Others may wish to maintain the current location within a village.

Still others may want to build a new facility within a small town on a small site and use offsite community locations for sports and other school functions. Thus, one main problem of acreage requirements is that state policies determine what school sites should look like, and may not reflect decisions made by the local community. Whether to relocate schools or keep them in existing locations should be a community decision.

Acreage policies place new and costly financial burdens on rural taxpayers. Acreage policies that require relocation of a school to a new site can be very costly for local communities. The most obvious additional costs for districts are for land and for the actual building. However, there are other "hidden" costs. These less obvious costs include expenses for infrastruc-tures such as roads for increased traffic, sewage systems, water and utility systems, and public services such as police and fire protection.

The costs of building large schools outside communi-ties are frequently underestimated because schools affect so many infrastructure services, and because they are funded by a variety of sources. A study of eight rural counties in states across the country uncovered a variety of costs and problems associated with building larger schools outside existing population centers.

These problems include congestion of transportation routes; the need to pave gravel roads; increased pollu-tion; the need to extend sewer systems; concerns about infrastructure costs affecting business growth; the decreasing supply of affordable housing; and the costs of public services such as police, fire and health. "A typical complaint was that police were too few to cover the area outside the municipalities, and volunteer fire departments were struggling to meet growing service needs".

Many communities have attempted to cover these

additional costs through impact fees for develop-ers, though this additional revenue does little to cover actual expenses. Although state aid may help with construction costs, expenses for infrastructure and services tend to be ongoing and are usually assumed by local taxpayers.

Acreage policies contribute to suburban sprawl and cause disruption or destruction of rural culture and livelihoods. Sprawl is often viewed as a suburban problem, but it is actually a rural issue. Typically, suburban sprawl results in rural areas being subsumed by expanding suburban communities. This issue has environmental, public health, economic and cultural implications that are beyond the scope of this issue brief. However, to the extent that acreage requirements encourage new schools to be located outside of existing population centers, they may be harbingers of sprawl.

In spite of a growing recognition of the benefits of small schools, many policies, either intentionally or unintentionally, create incentives to replace small school with larger ones. Policies that mandate or recommend minimum acreage for school sites are examples of these flawed policies.

The following recommendations suggest ways to rectify problems that impact rural and small schools from misguided acreage policies.

1. Eliminate Acreage Requirements

In the best-case scenario, state approval for school facility projects would not include acreage require-ments. There is no clear purpose for these require-ments, and these restrictions can be more harmful than beneficial, especially for small rural schools. States do help finance school building projects, and they should have some role in approving local projects.

However, state approval should be based on education-ally sound criteria.

2. Provide Exemptions from Acreage Requirements

If acreage guidelines remain, state policies should allow for exemptions, and the exemptions should be well publicized. Most states do permit exemptions to acreage minimums, though many of these exemptions are available only to urban schools, and many local education agencies operate as if unaware of these options. State policies can be written to be more explicit about exceptions to general recommendations and/or requirements.

There are a few good models of acreage policies with explicit exemptions. In Georgia, for example, though large sites are considered to be advantageous, the approval committee can grant a waiver for a school site in a high-density area. New York State recommenda-tions for acreage do not apply to New York City schools, and variances can be granted upon written request. Minnesota provides alternatives and different allowances for urban and rural schools.

North Carolina recognizes that urban districts may not be able to meet the recommendations, and Oklahoma recognizes that in urban places the cost of land may be prohibitive and the recommended acreage may be unrealistic. Policymakers must understand that acreage require-ments are an imposition on rural communities and that waivers must be available to all districts.

3. Redirect Growth

State policy can help guide new development in environmentally and educationally beneficial direc-tions. Some states direct construction of schools away from areas they want to protect and encourage renova-tion over new construction.

4. Encourage Renovation

In general, policies that favor construction of large new schools rather than renovation of older smaller facilities have disastrous impacts on small rural schools. There are, however, models for doing the opposite-encour-aging renovation. For example, Maryland encourages the reuse of existing buildings.

5. Form Partnerships

Much of the impetus for larger tracts of land for schools is probably the result of the desire and need for extensive athletic fields and parking. Sports teams are an important focus of civic pride and an excellent activity for many students; however, space for practice and competition need not dominate site decisions for schools. Furthermore, schools located closer to commu-nities need less space for bus and automobile parking than those cited in outlying areas.

Districts and the communities can form partnerships that are mutually beneficial, less costly, make better use of public resources, and avoid relocating schools onto large undeveloped land parcels removed from town centers. For example, students can use public parks, pools, playgrounds, athletic fields and other recre-ational areas if they are sited nearby.

Many schools already take advantage of this cost-cutting method. In a similar fashion, school facilities such as cafeterias, meeting rooms, media centers and libraries, gymnasiums, fitness centers, tracks, fields and pools can all be used by community people, who are often more likely to share in construction and mainte-nance expenses if they also share in the immediate benefits. Some states are beginning to encourage these partnerships.

Economic development is especially important to Tribal Colleges because of the historical problems with high rates of poverty and unemployment that have endured on the reservations on which they are located. It appears that poverty and unemployment rates are much higher among American Indians who live on reservations than among American Indians who live elsewhere.

Poverty in reservation communities has been accompanied by various social problems, such as alcohol and drug dependency, high incidence of diabetes and other diseases, and high rates of suicide. Furthermore, American Indians living on reservations historically have had low rates of educational attainment. At the same time, economic development on reservations would have a positive impact on the broader well-being of state, regional, and national economies.

One recent study revealed that Indian reservations, when considered as a group, have significant financial and job effects for non-reservation economies. Spending by reservation residents, tribal governments, and reservation-based businesses is estimated to create 300,000 jobs and $10 billion in wages and salary income in the national economy each year.

The majority of the almost 300 Indian reservations in the United States are located west of the Mississippi River in isolated rural areas. Almost 44 percent of the American Indian population lived in rural areas in 1990, compared to 25 percent of the total U.S. population. Because they are so concentrated, American Indians are particularly vulnerable to the economic problems faced by rural areas.

The economy of the American heartland has undergone great change in recent years, including deep recessions in agriculture and energy, restructuring in manufacturing, and the emergence of the service industry. Although some rural areas with scenic amenities or located in emerging trade centres have experienced recent growth, many areas remain in steep economic decline-especially farm-dependent and very remote areas.

In general, rural areas that have the potential to improve economically have lower labour and other business costs, better transportation, more doctors, more retirement activity, more colleges, and a better educated workforce. Unfortunately, many Indian reservations do not currently exhibit the characteristics necessary to improve their chances of economic growth.

There are many obstacles to economic development on reservations, including the following:

— *Low levels of education, shortages of skilled workers, and a lack of management expertise*

— *Limits regarding the use of reservation land held in trust by the federal government-property tax is not collected for such land, and the land cannot be used as collateral for loans*

— *Non-arable or poor-quality land, fragmented land ownership patterns, and frequently harsh climates*

—*Geographic isolation from major population centres*

—*Poorly developed physical infrastructures, such as transportation, water access, and utilities*

— *Lack of access to capital, as well as poorly developed institutional infrastructures in banking and financial services*

— *Low levels of investment by both insiders and outsiders*

— *Outsiders' lack of understanding of the sovereign immunity granted to tribal governments*

— *Need for consistent tribal regulations and policies toward business, across reservations and over time*

— *Long histories of exclusion, economic exploitation, and financial dependence on government welfare programs*

Reservations also have been impacted by larger trends in the American and world economies, including the movement of entry-level manufacturing jobs out of the country; the tendency of industries to cluster, as illustrated by Silicon Valley; and the growing use of just-in-time delivery, which depends on regular, rapid access to parts and materials. These trends affect tribal communities, which are somewhat dependent on the economic circumstances of surrounding communities.

The broader trends also may compound obstacles such as the lack of rural transportation networks; for example, a lack of easy access to highways and other transport systems not only is a huge barrier to getting jobs, but also renders just in time delivery nearly impossible.

The Rural Community College Initiative (RCCI) is a national demonstration project that aims to help community colleges in specific distressed rural areas to expand access to postsecondary education and help foster regional economic development. To accomplish this goal, the Initiative hopes to strengthen rural community colleges by enhancing their capacity to provide economic leadership for their regions and serve as agents for community development.

Each participating college-which includes nine pilot colleges and 15 other institutions-receives an initial grant to support the development of plans by representatives from both the college and the community, followed by modest implementation grants, annual institutes, and on-site consulting. RCCI is a partnership of the Ford Foundation, the American Association of Community Colleges, MDC, Inc., the American

Council on Education, and the participating colleges.

In particular, micro-enterprises may form the basis of future economic development on the reservations, and can be supported by the colleges through entrepreneurship courses, degree programs, and technical assistance.

The Rural Empowerment Zone and Enterprise Community (EZ/EC) Program, sponsored primarily by the U.S. Departments of Agriculture (USDA) and Housing and Urban Development (HUD), is designed to provide communities with real opportunities for growth and revitalization. The program has four guiding principles: the creation of jobs is the foundation for economic self-sufficiency; sustainable development can only be successful if job creation and other efforts are integrated into a comprehensive strategy that includes physical and human development; all segments of the community must participate in development efforts, and partnerships must be formed with and among the various levels of government; and a bold vision for change is necessary to create a strategic plan for revitalization.

The Community Empowerment Program was enacted in 1993. In 1994, communities with high rates of poverty applied in the first round of the program, and three rural Empowerment Zones and 30 rural Enterprise Communities were named. Indian reservation lands became eligible for the second round of the program, which in 1998 established five new rural Empowerment Zones and 20 rural Enterprise Communities.

Empowerment Zones and Enterprise Communities are eligible for varying combinations of grants, tax benefit packages, flexibility in overcoming regulatory requirements, and other benefits. In addition, they may receive special consideration in competition for funding through some federal programs. Many of these features combine to deter even routine investment in Indian Country. For example, between 1992 and 1996, lenders made only 91 conventional home loans to American Indians on trust lands. In addition, such obstacles discourage businesses from locating on or near reservations.

The larger businesses that do exist on reservations tend to be established with federal or tribal money or are involved in natural resources extraction. Because tribal governments have been under pressure to maximize employment, the primary purpose of tribal-owned businesses-particularly in the past-was to provide jobs rather than to be profitable. At the same time, small businesses offering basic services such as groceries may be scarce, and small business entrepreneurs must deal with a shortage of venture capital and start-up money, and a relative lack of technical and managerial advice.

Despite recent economic growth on and around some reservations, tribal wealth remains uneven, and economic development has not necessarily translated into improvements in jobs and economic well-being for all communities. Jobs are scarce due to the small size and isolation of many reservations, and a substantial proportion of reservation residents do not even participate in the labour force. The jobs that do exist on reservations tend to be in the public sector-for example, major employers are federal and tribal governments, schools, and the U.S. Public Health Service.

In contrast, American Indians are much more likely to be employed in general services, agriculture, forestry, or fishing. Like the economic circumstances prevalent in IndianCountry overall, the reservations served by Tribal Colleges tend to have high rates of poverty and unemployment. The unemployment rate of American Indians living on Tribal College reservations averaged 42 percent in 1995, and was as high as 77 per-cent on the Cheyenne River Sioux reservation in South Dakota, home of Cheyenne River Community College.

Yet unemployment rates do not account for adults who

are no longer looking for work and have left the labour force. Looking at the potential labour force, the average percent who are not employed increases to 62 percent, and was reported to be 95 percent on the Rosebud Sioux reservation in South Dakota, on which Sinte Gleska University is located. In comparison, the U.S. population as a whole had an unemployment rate of about 6 percent in 1995, and an estimated 37 percent of the potential labour force who were not employed.

The average per capita income on Tribal College reservations was only $4,665, while the average per capita income for the U.S. population overall was $19,188 in 1990. On the Pine Ridge Reservation in South Dakota, home of Oglala Lakota College, more than 70 percent of residents do not have jobs. The main business on the reservation is a gas station, and many homes in the community do not have running water or telephones. The area has been called the poorest census tract in the nation.

Given the importance of education to raising the levels of income and employment, one can see how important higher education institutions-and Tribal Colleges in particular-will be to the future development of reservation communities. Tribal Colleges' development efforts share important similarities with those of many different kinds of postsecondary institutions. For example, community colleges contribute to the development of local communities in specific ways:

— *Direct spending and employment. Community colleges, their students, and their employees make various purchases that contribute to demand in the local economy. In addition, the colleges directly create many jobs.*

— *Workforce development. Through their instruction, they increase the skills of local workers, which in turn increases the employment and earnings opportunities of these workers.*

Generally, community colleges tailor their programs to meet specific local needs, and their curricula tend to change continuously to reflect shifting needs.

— *Business attraction. The development of local human capital leads to increases in local productivity. By increasing the skills of the local workforce-as well as performing community impact studies and other activities-community colleges encourage business and industry to locate in the region.*

— *Small business and entrepreneurship development. In many reservation communities, local entrepreneurs wanting to start their own small businesses need help in understanding and surmounting the challenges they face. Community colleges also serve entrepreneurs by providing business development expertise through technical assistance, the operation of Small Business Development Centres, incubation services, and specially targeted programs.*

Approximately 40 percent of community colleges in small communities and rural areas operate Small Business Development Centres. In addition, a small number are involved in business incubators-facilities in which shared services and management assistance are provided for tenant companies, usually in exchange for rent, fees, a percentage of sales revenue, or equity in the company.

— *Technology transfer. Community colleges also can contribute to the development of physical capital by applying their research expertise-by demonstrating new technologies, serving as information clearinghouses on new technologies, or other innovation-related activities.*

— *Leadership. Community college leaders play a major role in making a public commitment to economic development, and in creating public awareness of the importance of college programs and activities to future growth.*

— *Linkages. Community colleges act as leaders to open up the lines of communication between public education, social services, four-year colleges, and the business community. "Especially in distressed areas, the community college is often the institution best capable of initiating and nurturing the local partnerships and regional collaborations that can help solve critical community problems".*

Tribal Colleges are perhaps most comparable to rural community colleges, which are more likely to operate with lower levels of resources than other community colleges or four-year institutions but tend to take on a more expansive role in community development. "In rural areas, the local community college is the only game in town for economic development, cultural enrichment, and higher education".

Thus, rural community colleges traditionally play a dominant role in the community, and may be the "primary catalyst for improving the quality of rural life". Although the resources of Tribal Colleges tend to be even lower than those of most rural community colleges, Tribal Colleges are similar in their significance for the local community. As new land-grant institutions, Tribal Colleges also have become part of a specific tradition of involvement in economic development.

Like community colleges, land-grant universities have been formally involved in rural economic development for many decades. According to a survey by the National Association of State Universities and Land-Grant Colleges (NASULGC), land-grant universities foster new business and create long-term job growth; promote innovation; enhance the workforce; and conduct research at the forefront of sustainable agriculture in order to improve the quality of rural life. They therefore perform many of the same activities as community colleges, and often work in cooperation with nearby community colleges in local development efforts.

Tribal Colleges also share experiences with other minority-serving institutions. Historically Black Colleges and Universities (HBCUs), for example, took on the responsibility of improving the economic well-being of African Americans from their earliest stages, and appear to be better at preparing African American students for professional life than predominantly white institutions. Research has shown that attendance at HBCUs has human capital development benefits that lead to higher wages in the labour market.

Like Tribal Colleges, HBCUs have faced barriers to their involvement with economic development that are specific to their role as minority-serving institutions, including: limitations in their curricula due to historic underfunding; exclusion from many informal social networks; and perceived or real effects of racial bias. Tribal Colleges contribute to local development in numerous ways that are similar to efforts of other postsecondary institutions.

At the same time, they add two unique aspects. First, Tribal Colleges integrate cultural relevance into their development efforts, as tribal traditions and values permeate the curricula and learning styles of the colleges. This ability of the colleges fits in with the broad vision of economic development in which higher education institutions become "community-building colleges," empowering their local communities to create sustainable economic activities while preserving traditional cultural values.

Second, Tribal Colleges have a special responsibility to help local communities understand the nature of choices between different types of economic growth, given the specific history of economic development on reservations. For example, job creation may mean reliance on one industry to provide a steady supply of jobs (as it has in the past), or it may mean a dynamic expansion of the economy with new jobs and businesses;

Tribal Colleges can illuminate the disparate impacts of these types of development on the long-term health of the community. Both of these special aspects of Tribal Colleges' contributions to local economic development support the future success of such efforts.

In general, the Tribal Colleges have both direct and long-term impacts on local economies. Direct effects result from the dollars spent and circulated into the economy, and come through several mechanisms: spending by the institution, employees, students, and even visitors; jobs, including college employees and jobs created by college spending; and the provision of services to the local community.

The long-term effects result from the completion of a college's mission, and include the following: workforce development; fostering entrepreneurship and small business growth; initiation and dissemination of new research; and promoting efficiency and environmentally sound practices in agriculture and natural resources (NASULGC).

Arguably, the long-term impacts of Tribal Colleges on their local communities may be even more important to local economic development than the direct economic effects, as they help communities establish a foundation for future growth. In comparison, rural community colleges overall spent an average of $6.3 million on employee compensation in that year (NCES). Meanwhile, employees, visitors, and students spend money for such things as transportation, food, and other living expenses.

When employees, visitors, and students are from outside the local community or when the purchases are financed with external financial aid, such spending represents new expenditures that directly result from the colleges' existence. In turn, both of these types of spending stimulate activity in the local economy. Because they hire a significant number of local residents, Tribal Colleges serve as important employers in the community.

In addition to teaching, college employees may be involved in a variety of occupational activities, including administrative positions, professional, clerical, and technical support, skilled crafts, and service/maintenance positions. It is also important to note that at the tribally controlled colleges 57 percent of employees were American Indian, compared to 3 percent at rural community colleges overall. The percentage varied according to position- 76 percent of full-time staff were American Indian, compared to 26 percent of full-time faculty.

Finally, Tribal Colleges provide essential services to local residents, businesses, and tribal governments. Such public service activities include continuing education and GED courses, health and counseling clinics, library services, cultural programs, management of public housing, and provision of catering services to students, Head Start programs, and even local prisons.

Tribal Colleges often are useful to the tribal leadership by analyzing various economic trends and other factors that will influence the tribal economy. In addition, they can serve as focal points for local development initiatives, providing coordination and leadership.

Tribal Colleges can play a critical role in economic development in Indian Country by thoroughly preparing the next generation of managers and entrepreneurs. Tribal Colleges encourage workforce development in several ways: they match their curricula with local needs; they increase the overall skill levels-and commensurate earnings-of the local labour force; and they contribute to higher rates of employment by graduating students who are then employed within the community.

Tribal Colleges offer a range of courses that are specific to local communities' needs. Program developers have been careful to create programs that produce graduates with high employability in local markets. Many Tribal Colleges offer degrees in such fields as social service, secretarial skills, and early childhood education to address manpower needs in tribal agencies, day care centres, Head Start programs, and other government sponsored activities.

Tribal Colleges offer programs in other marketable areas, such as nursing, computer-related technologies, and electronics technologies, which were considered the "hot" community college programs in 1997. According to a survey of Tribal College students, business was the most common field of study, followed by health professions, education, and vocational/ technical trades.

Through the teaching of their curricula, Tribal Colleges increase the skills and productivity levels of their students. In turn, this leads to higher earnings for their students, and thus for the community as a whole. One recent study attempted to measure these effects by examining economic indicators for Tribal College reservations compared to similar reservations without Tribal Colleges. It indicated a positive correlation between Tribal Colleges and both workers' incomes and significantly lower poverty rates.

Over the past few decades, median income for males and females grew at faster rates on Tribal College reservations than on the reservations without Tribal Colleges. For example, between 1980 and 1990 the growth in female median income was 49 percent greater on Tribal College reservations than on reservations without Tribal Colleges.

Between 1980 and 1990, overall poverty rates grew 22

percent more on the reservations without Tribal Colleges, and family poverty increased 8 percent more. Thus, reservations with Tribal Colleges appear to have improved their economic circumstances more than similar reservations without Tribal Colleges have. The results hold even when accounting for the broader influence of states' economic progress.

In addition, there appeared to be a positive relationship between the number of years each Tribal College had been in existence and most of the income measures. All of these findings suggest that Tribal Colleges are directly impacting the economic health of their local communities. Because of the relatively high rates of participation in postsecondary education on many Tribal College reservations, these institutions have the potential to significantly improve the skills and earnings of a substantial proportion of local residents.

For all reservation-based, tribally controlled colleges that serve primarily students from their own reservation, 4 percent of the American Indian residents ages 16 to 64 were enrolled in fall 1995-and in some states, the percentage was 10 percent or more. This suggests that a significant proportion of adults were participating in a Tribal College education in some way during that semester, and an even greater proportion have taken Tribal College courses over many years.

This compares favourably with the slightly less than 3 percent of the population 18 years and older who were served by all community colleges in the same semester. At the same time, this participation has a multi-generational effect the children of Tribal College graduates will be more likely to attend college, thereby encouraging continuing development of the workforce in the future.

In addition to improved skills and higher earnings, Tribal Colleges' efforts in workforce development appear to lead to higher rates of employment. Although national data are not currently available, some specific examples suggest that Tribal College graduates are performing significantly better than tribal members who have not attended, in terms of their rates of employment and continuing education.

Many of the colleges provide employment or placement services to their students; others, however, do not have the resources to staff such services, and must use more informal mechanisms such as community networks. The employment of graduates is especially important because so many graduates remain in the community.

In some cases, graduates develop skills and abilities that allow them to take local positions that were once held by non-tribal members. However, Tribal Colleges' education and training is also part of the larger process of job creation and expansion of the local economy. When jobs do not exist, many graduates may utilize their Tribal College experiences to create their own jobs through micro-enterprise and other forms of entrepreneurship. Thus, the employment of graduates in the community is linked closely with Tribal Colleges' efforts to encourage the growth of small business and entrepreneurship.

Tribal Colleges promote long-term economic growth by providing instruction and technical assistance to local business owners and potential entrepreneurs. By doing this, they recognize that the key to economic growth lies not only in unproved training and education on the reservations, but also in the encouragement of large numbers of small enterprises that are owned and managed by American Indian entrepreneurs.

A survey conducted in the 1980s revealed the value of micro-enterprises on the Pine Ridge Reservation: such businesses provided income for 87 percent of the households, and 30 percent of responding households indicated that at least half of total household income came from self-employment activity. At the same time, many reservations are in dire need of more local services, such as car repair and retail outlets.

Thus, small business development presents one of the greatest opportunities for economic growth. Tribal Colleges help relieve two of the main barriers for American Indian businesses: credit availability and management skills. Tribal Colleges offer broader training and education to reservation communities, including an increased emphasis on business and entrepreneurism. The colleges promote entrepreneurship and small bushiness growth through courses, workshops, leadership developments, and technical assistance via small business centres.

Since its inception in 1969, United Tribes Technical College (UTTC) has served multiple tribes in economic development. Since then, UTTC has sponsored numerous conferences and summits in the area of development, bringing together many different tribes to plan for the future. In general, UTTC encourages economic development in several capacities: providing technical assistance to numerous tribes on the Northern Plains as well as American Indian individuals; serving as an intertribal forum for policy and program discussions; and offering specific kinds of training that are part of its mission.

In 1980, the college created an Indian Business Development Center, operated under memoranda of agreement with the Administration for Native Americans, the Bureau of Indian Affairs, and the Department of Commerce's Minority Business Development Agency (which continues to fund the effort). Now called the United Tribes ND/SD Native American Business Development Center, the center promotes the self-sufficiency of American Indian businesses, provides procurement services and specialized training, and offers management and technical assistance.

Between 1988 and 1998, the center provided more than $17 million of assistance in the form of prepared financial packages and almost $29 million in procurement of new contracts for clients. As economic development is linked to the quality of civic leadership, Tribal Colleges also try to strengthen leadership skills.

The Tribal Colleges are also promoting entrepreneurship and small business development through innovative support centres that provide technical assistance. Almost a third of the colleges currently have Tribal Business Information Centres (TBICs), which are funded by the U.S. Small Business Administration (SBA).

The TBICs provide help to both students and the wider community with business plans, budgets, marketing, and other activities. Other colleges support small bushiness through similar centers that are funded by the colleges themselves, or through other sources. For example:

Northwest Indian College of Bellingham, Washington has been supporting local entrepreneurs since 1988 through its Business Assistance Center, which provides access to expert advice on business planning and operation. Clients come to the center looking for help in preparing a business plan they can present to banks and government agencies for financing. Other clients already have successful businesses, but require assistance in more specific areas such as inventory control, marketing research, or personnel management. In addition to the main campus site, Northwest also has Business Assistance Centers at its instructional sites on seven other reservations in Washington state.

Land use and resource development on Tribal College reservations represent another long-term economic impact, as the colleges contribute to improved agricultural and natural resource management practices. "Land tenure is one of the most complicated issues affecting Indian economic development, not only in the sense that it is an economic asset, but also because it is the wellspring of tribal identity and preservation".

Overall, American Indian land remains in high demand due to abundant agricultural, timber, and mineral resources. However, "most tribes do not have the capital, technology, or expertise to develop these resources". In addition, these resources are distributed unevenly among reservations and tribes. As a result of the General Allotment Act of 1887, tribal land-holdings overall were reduced by two-thirds and land was distributed in individual parcels to both Indians and non-Indians, resulting in a checkerboard pattern of ownership that limits many economic development opportunities.

The system of dividing ownership shares equally among heirs exacerbated the situation and made it virtually impossible for Indian landowners to assemble enough land to make agricultural operations profitable. In addition, before the 1970s the federal government was the de facto manager of American Indians' land, and federal development and spending priorities often conflicted with tribal priorities. Since then, land use policies have changed, and increasing levels of education have given reservation residents the skills needed to protect their interests.

Today, tribes have substantial-but not complete-control over the development of surface, underground, and water resources on their reservations. Tribal land constitutes a major source of income for many tribes, involving revenue from farming, timber, grazing, and industrial leasing. Nevertheless, there are various obstacles and issues involved in the use of tribal land, many of which must be resolved as part of any economic development process.

Agriculture remains the dominant use for American Indian land, although its importance is decreasing due to both broader trends in the rural economy and problems specific to the reservations. The continued lack of available farming credit and adequate irrigation remain serious obstacles to successful agricultural enterprises, and non-Indians farming or ranching on tribally owned lands are a frequent occurrence.

At the same time, agriculture in the United States is changing enormously, with significant impacts on Tribal College reservations. Farms are getting bigger and fewer, the global market for farm products is shifting, and federal farm programs are being scaled back. Although agriculture will remain the mainstay of communities that historically have depended upon it, those ties will change and communities will need to adapt. Reservation communities will need to rethink their approach to agriculture entirely-traditional uses of the land are not always the best, and communities need to expand their portfolio of options.

Meanwhile, tribal land overall contains nearly six million acres of sustainable commercial timberland, and the potential for income and employment from mining is significant for the few reservations with mineral resources. Natural resource management for tribes has generally involved the concept of sustainable development-a combination of economic development and the consumption of natural resources in sustainable ways.

In other words, reservation resources are managed with the realization that they are finite, and the resource potential must be preserved. The issue of sustainable development has been the focus of many tribes, including some on Tribal College reservations.

Internet Access in Rural Areas

Today, stakeholders are beginning to recognize the political and economic significance of the more than half of the world's population that lives in largely untapped rural markets. Governments and nongovernmental organizations are increasingly concerned with addressing economic development goals and stability, stubborn deficits in rural health and learning, urban migration, environmental degradation, and other related trends.

The private sector craves new consumers, producers, ideas, and synergies in our rapidly globalizing environment. What most have yet to understand, however, are the tremendous opportunities to address these challenges through new information and information communication technologies (ICTs).

Increasingly powerful, flexible, and economical, ICTs present staggering new opportunities for social and economic integration. Achieving the promise of ICTs does not require sacrifice on the part of business, government, or civil society, but it does demand their vision, cooperation, and action to create the environment and mechanisms necessary for ICTs to flourish in the rural areas of the developing world.

One force necessary-albeit insufficient-for the establishment of pervasive and sustainable readiness for the Networked World, especially in developing and rural areas, is the market. It is commonly assumed that effective rural ICT access requires economic subsidy and financial loss; however, ICTs should be economically viable if they are to gain wide, robust, and long-lived usage.

While the path to realizing such economics will vary

across countries, settings, cultures, and technologies, consider one critical issue: Internet for rural regions of developing nations. In researching and studying the economic self-sustainability of the Internet in rural areas, we have identified some criteria for success-something of a laundry list. This list suggests that there are at least six broad categories that must be considered for economic self-sustainability: costs, revenue, networks, business models, policy, and capacity.

The groupings are imperfect due to the interrelationship and interdependence among categories, which make consideration of any one category ineffective. A more accurate way to think of the categories might be to imagine them as a balloon, which when pushed in one area, bulges in others. For instance, policy will affect cost, which in turn influences business models and therefore revenue and on down the line; this leads us to the not-so-profound conclusion that everything affects everything else.

We have artificially isolated the relationships between some of the diverse factors affecting economic sustainability for rural Internet, but it should be noted only when the system is taken as a whole can we describe it accurately. One important assumption underlying many issues in the effort to achieve self-sustainable Internet service is that, in a poor rural setting, the Internet is likely for some time to be delivered as a community resource, rather than a personal one.

In other words, rather than each individual having a network-enabled digital appliance for himself or herself, each village or community might have shared resources that are financially sustained through some combination of user fees and outside revenue. This basic model is often realized through some form of community access point for information and communications services, often known as a community telecenter or telekiosk.

Telecenters in the developing world have, been primarily sponsored and undertaken by governments, multilateral institutions, and nonprofits. Because of the desire to create what is essentially a public good (access to information and communications services), only secondary attention has been paid to entrepreneurism and sustainable business.

There have been significant achievements under challenging circumstances, but generally we have been better at learning about and making mistakes with telecenters than we have been at creating economically sustainable models and universal access to ICT in rural areas. At present, the most significant capital costs in offering community Internet are for hardware and network access equipment. A range of low cost Internet-enabled digital appliances have been developed, and these can be far cheaper, and indeed, better adapted to the developing world context in their form and function, than traditional desktop computers.

While they remain the dominant access device, personal computers (PCs) are inappropriate for the developing world across many dimensions, due to relatively high cost, low reliability, unsuitable user interface, environmental sensitivity, and high power consumption. Handheld appliances such as the Simputer or Pengachu have shown that network-enabled computers can today be priced at under US$300. Longer-term research, at the Massachusetts Institute of Technology (MIT) Media Laboratory and elsewhere, prices next generation appliances at dollars or even pennies.

Additional high fixed costs are due to the network infrastructure. Connections achieved via the public switched telephone network (PSTN) often carry high fixed costs. Both fixed and mobile wireless technologies fundamentally change cost structure because they reduce the time, effort, and expense of last mile service delivery, which typically comprises the majority of all infrastructure costs. Moreover, wireless allows new entrants to compete against incumbent providers with their own facilities, and the operator has an increased incentive to maximize the number of users because the marginal cost for each additional user is lower than with wireline networks.

New low-cost network technologies are fundamentally rewriting equations of economic self-sustainability for rural Internet connectivity. Those rural communities within microwave radio reach of existing fibber optic cable links can effectively make use of Wireless Local Loop (WLL) last mile solutions. At today's price of under US$300 per subscriber line, WLL solutions such as the corDECT technology can provide both telephone and Internet connectivity up to 10 km away from the base station, and 25 km from a relay base station.

The corDECT system is engineered primarily for low price, rather than added (and often unnecessary) features, and is therefore designed for developing world needs. The system offers 35.5/70 Kbps simultaneous voice/data transmission. For rural communities too distant from fiber backbones or in terrain too rough for the line of sight required between terrestrial microwave antennas, Very Small Aperture Terminal (VSAT) satellite is a common approach for connectivity.

Today's prices for send/receive units range from about US$4,000 to over US$10,000, thus making this approach inappropriate for many poor or small communities. VHF or UHF wireless solutions are a potentially compelling option for narrowband connectivity that can also function in remote and rough terrain, or relatively depopulated, settings. These can cost under US$800 per subscriber line, transmit over 200 km distances, and provide upwards of 9.6 Kbps connectivity.

The main factors contributing to recurrent costs include

telephone, Internet access, power, and personnel costs. These costs are primarily related to issues of government policy and competitive environments, and to the extent that they directly affect economic sustainability. Telephone toll charges can make up a heavy percentage of recurrent costs if a regular telephone call is necessary to connect to the Internet, particularly given the prevalence of time-metered calling and Internet Service Providers (ISP) that require long-distance calls.

Telephone and Internet access technologies that separate voice and data, such as the corDECT system, can reduce costs by handing voice off to the PSTN while switching data directly to an ISP. Such a simple technological accommodation that does not bill Internet access as a phone call can allow substantial savings in telephone toll charges, and does so in the absence of a policy decision that bills Internet at a different rate or offers flat rate calling.

Research suggests that for both power and Internet charges, costs for solar photovoltaic (PV) power and wireless connectivity will incur lower recurrent operating costs as compared to grid power sources and wireline connectivity. Indeed, when amortized over a period of years, the savings in operating costs will make up for the added capital costs. In other words, being off the electricity grid does not necessarily imply higher net present valuation.

Moreover, due to the fact that grid power is commonly unreliable in the developing world, backup power supplies and batteries imply additional costs and frustration that can be reduced under systems such as solar PV. It should be noted that alternative energy supplies may have implications for related electrical infrastructure, such as air conditioning or photocopiers. More compelling than PV power or other renewable sources, however, are new advances in very low-power consuming digital appliances.

Similar to the well-known wind-up radio, wind-up Internet appliances are genuine technological options. Finally, in an assessment of rural Internet services for Tamil Nadu in India, McKinsey & Company-Delhi has argued that recurrent costs can be reduced by 30 percent in rent, electric power, and salaries if the service is provided within an existing business. Commonly observed examples include telephone call centers, temples, small grocery stores, schools, post offices, and government offices. Depending on the local labour market, availability and competitive remuneration for qualified employees varies widely.

One commonly observed strategy for telecenters is to hire secondary and tertiary students at low wages to serve as facilitators and perform other tasks such as repair and research, and to make the position more appealing by offering free Internet access. With today's technologies, a village in India can be brought online and provisioned with Internet, telephone service, a computer, and so on, for under US$1,000 in capital costs and with ongoing recurrent costs approaching US$60 per month.

It is likely that these figures can be reduced by an order of magnitude over the next decade. It goes without saying, however, that costs are intimately related with other aspects of the community and business model, including culture, geography, population density, services, technologies, and other factors, and that their interaction will dictate observed cost.

If equipment, connections, rent, and salaries, are the economic pains needed to offer rural Internet service, user fees for applications and remote services, and income resulting from the aggregation of many users are the economic gains. Given that the technology components and public access business model is essentially a platform capable of facilitating a wide range of activities, more applications and content will allow revenue generation from a greater variety of sources and effectively lower the level of income necessary for the sustainability of each unique application.

There will also be associated benefits arising from the wider and deeper integration of the telecenter and ICTs within the community. User fees are particularly difficult to generate in some cases, they are not the only source of income. User fees, however, yield other benefits besides the generation of financial support; they also ensure economical use of the infrastructure and offer a market incentive and feedback for content, applications, and services that are appropriate to the users in that community.

User fees generate challenges, however. A market mechanism may lead to externalities that some consider negative, including the development and diffusion of games, adult content, and other potentially controversial applications. It may result in unequal access for different members of the community, such as children and (particularly) poor people, who may require subsidies or discounts to address their needs effectively.

There are three main classes of revenue production for rural Internet services. First is fee-for-services such as core communications, education, commerce, government applications, entertainment, training, and so forth. Second is a variety of remote services and back office activities. Finally, the aggregation of services and users provide opportunities for revenue.

Core Communication Applications

Core communication services are the killer applications, acting as a pathway to other uses of information and communication technology. This was true in the nations of the Organisation for Economic Co-operation and Development (OECD) and in urban areas, and it will be true in the rural South. In other words, the core revenue generators are information systems that connect people to each other despite barriers of time, distance, written literacy, and ownership of a telephone or computer.

Synchronous and asynchronous text and voice services such as e-mail, voice mail, chat, and Voice over Internet Protocol (Internet telephony or VoIP) are particularly relevant in many developing world contexts. This is due to commonly observed characteristics such as high call charges (relative to both income levels and comparable rates in the OECD), high rates of national and international migration, weak postal systems, and limited direct access to communications devices (i.e., like a telephone in the home).

With public Internet access sometimes costing less per hour than a local telephone call (and much less than the exorbitant long distance rates), e-mail, chat, voice mail, and VoIP are appealing cost savings measures. In Peru, for instance, rates for public Internet access are often less than US$0.50 per hour, while telephone card rates for local calls are approximately US$0.60 per hour; long distance costs US$0.80 per minute and upwards, as compared to less than US$0.20 for VoIP calls. Note that VoIP is illegal in many countries.

These text and voice services have been shown to be strong revenue sources for those providing access to Internet services in rural areas. In rural Bangladesh, for instance, International Telecommunications Union (ITU) models argue that not less than 1.5 percent of Gross Domestic Product (GDP) per capita will be spent on core communication services, while estimates for India suggest communications spending of up to 5 to 6 percent of GDP per capita.

Early Internet trends in Bangladesh show that 82 percent of the online traffic is going to e-mail. Thus, in Bangladesh, there is both the demand and willingness to pay for communication services and these services seem to comprise the majority of Internet usage. As trends toward increased labour mobility continue and agricultural production becomes more linked to urban markets, rural "organic communication networks" and and their communication demands will only expand further. Communication is both a core desire of most communities and a relatively straightforward process to support with the use of ICTs.

Whereas, for instance, designing a Web interface to manage a supply chain and integrate it into business can be quite complex, voice and text communications applications, being fairly simple and requiring minimal localization, can quickly begin running in communities. While many applications are already available, additional innovations in core communication applications are required if user demands in rural areas are to be fully satisfied.

The MIT Media Lab, for instance, has been exploring new multiliterate keyboard-less systems that support threaded voice discussion for new VoIP systems particularly suited for rural areas in developing countries. These new technologies, and business models to deliver them, are designed to flourish in rural developing areas by fulfilling the unique needs of their communities and networks.

At least 50 percent (and possibly much more in the early stages of connectivity) of revenue from user fees for rural Internet services will arise from the provision of core communication services. These services will enable people to better address their basic needs to communicate with family, with remote trading partners, with their government or others.

E-commerce, e-government, entertainment, education, and health show promise for additional specific applications and services that reach beyond basic communication. These areas only to evaluate how they might provide additional services based on user fees. E-commerce for rural developing areas has often been seen as a problem of porting the existing e-commerce models of the OECD, framed by concepts such as "B2B," electronic payment systems, and so on.

E-commerce environments must offer different services and employ alternative delivery and exchange mechanisms, and they must provide relevant and worthwhile support to the agricultural, informal, and micro- and small business sectors. Private sector groups are also interested in other potential commercial applications including insurance sales, remittance transmission, and other financial services.

These groups pursue their goals in the face of subsistence economies, little access to capital, no credit cards, and the absence of effective tools for consumer protection and dispute resolution. The case of agribusiness and agricultural management support systems has been given considerable attention in the ICT and development community. And indeed, there appears to be scope for agricultural services based on user-fees.

However, although market price information for the agricultural sector is often touted as a substantial value addition of rural Internet services, the promise and economic self-sustainability of such a service has recently been called into question. Market prices can be valuable, but their importance will depend on other community characteristics including availability of transport, credit, and alternative markets.

E-government services can also support economic self-sustain-ability via user fees. In the Gyandoot project of Dhar district, India, a collection of telekiosks run by local operators offer e-government services to consumer-citizens. A study of one such telekiosk showed that the grievance system, a facility for citizens to lodge complaints against the government with a guaranteed response within one week, was the third most popular information service of the program.

Entertainment, as it relates to rural Internet service, is a fundamental application area that has not been sufficiently studied. One indicator of the power of entertainment content, however, is the penetration of cable television into rural India. In India there are roughly 32 million cable television subscribers as compared, for instance, to 26 million fixed telephone subscribers. In rural India there are at least 10.5 million cable subscribers, making up 32.5 percent of the country's total subscription base and 8 percent of all rural households.

Small, independently operated businesses provide cable television in rural villages at a cost of only dollars per month. Clearly, rural cable TV is economically self-sustainable, indeed is flourishing, given the large demand and willingness to pay for entertainment products in rural and poor India, and the reasonably low costs. Furthermore, the entire existing cable network was rolled out in less than a decade.

Education and health are critical application areas if the Internet is to directly address core development objectives in rural areas, and they also can help with economic self-sustainability through powerful public-private collaborations. The World Links project, for instance, has been developing an after-school community telecenter program in Uganda.

Under this program, schools in rural Uganda that are equipped with computer labs and VSAT-based Internet connections are opening up their labs to outside clients in the afternoons and evenings on a cost-recovery basis. Funds are then used to cross-subsidize daytime educational use. In other words, educational use of the Internet has become economically self-sustaining by leveraging the existing school infrastructure, all the while allowing the surrounding community to benefit from ICTs; the outside community, in turn, supports the educational mission of the computer laboratory. Similar creative partnerships with rural health clinics have been envisioned.

Furthermore, delivery of training, in particular computer training, is increasingly in high demand for rural Internet centers. NIIT, a multinational computer training and service corporation, has franchised five hundred thirty rural ICT training facilities situated in villages throughout India. These facilities offer mostly basic and short-term training in computer literacy, Microsoft products, and so forth. These rural ICT training facilities educate forty to fifty students per year in small laboratories, and are operating as financially viable businesses.

ICT-enabled Services

A variety of remote services and back office activities may be performed anywhere and delivered anywhere, given adequate Internet connectivity and available people with the relevant communications capacity (primarily literacy in the appropriate language) and skill set (ranging widely from accounting to medicine to ICT problem solving). Spryance, an India-based remote services company with headquarters in the United States, has developed a pioneering home and rural medical transcription program that allows people with an adequate connection to the Internet in any part of the globe, to participate in the knowledge economy.

Spryance employees, mostly women, work out of their own homes, providing transcription services over the Internet.

The program has been growing at a rate of 25 percent per month over the last year and average earnings are more than twice those of comparable "factory-style" environments. While the home-based workforce program started mostly in metropolitan areas, it continues to expand into submetropolitan and rural areas.

A variety of network effects will drive economic self-sustain-ability of rural Internet. The number of Internet users overall, and particularly those in rural areas and developing nations, are an important factor in its sustainability-not only because they will pay user fees, but because of their effect on others. That is, each additional user increases the value of the network to all other users quadratically, offering more opportunities for interaction, seeding incentives for content, and service creation, all the while sharing the infrastructure cost burden more broadly.

Metcalfe Effect

Bob Metcalfe, inventor of the Ethernet, has identified a critical type of network effect which now bears his name. The Metcalfe Effect argues that the value of any complete network such as the Internet (where all things connected to the network have access to all other things) grows with the square of the number of users, as opposed to a simple linear growth. Put simply, the Metcalfe Effect tells two things. One is that the value of the Internet grows very quickly with the number of users, but, conversely, the value of the network is quite small when there are a small number of users connected.

The Metcalfe Effect suggests that the value to users, and thus self-sustaining demand for the network, will only be substantial when a sufficient number of interrelated groups are connected. As long as rural Internet connections are left to isolated pilot projects or small scale efforts-one here and one there-they will never leverage the Metcalfe Effect and the real value of the Internet.

When entire rural regions are networked, so as to connect communities to their neighbours, families, friends, governments, markets, and intermediaries, regardless of where they are, true value can be delivered. In addition to creating value for users, this aggregation of users, their needs, and the integration of their markets, provides another attractive source of revenue.

Much as a magazine becomes increasingly interesting to advertisers and contributing writers as its circulation rises, even a rural user community becomes a viable market for outside organizations, in the public, private, and non-profit sectors. Prahalad and Hart have shown that fast-moving consumer goods (FMCGs) manufacturers can gain a great deal by attending to rural, poor markets previously thought to provide no opportunity. Because reaching these consumers can be challenging, Indian firms, such as detergent makers Nirma and Hindustan Lever, are interested in and willing to pay for enhanced access to those populations via the Internet.

Agricultural firms are similarly interested. EID Parry is an Indian firm that manufactures and markets fertilizer, among other activities, and has been providing Internet kiosks to their sugar farmer customers in Nellikuppam, in rural Tamil Nadu. These facilities help EID Parry reach out to local growers, offering them technical assistance and information, developing new sales opportunities, and providing logistical support and credit services. Their online Cane Management System, which offers farmers a personalized account, including details on their fertilizer needs, outstanding credit to EID Parry, acreage, and so forth, has proven to be their most popular service.

Thus, fee-for-service on applications is not the only possible revenue model for the Internet in rural areas. Access to users can be provided for a fee to outside businesses, while respecting privacy and protecting communities. Agricultural companies, FMCG companies, the government, NGOs, and the like, all have an interest in these aggregations. But the value comes only when enough members of the target community and enough communities are aggregated. Returning to the magazine analogy, increased circulation, prestige, and certain demographics will motivate contributors.

By the same token, a sufficiently attractive userbase can also offer an incentive for content to be generated and applications designed for them, thus potentially creating additional value and revenues for telekiosks. Rural Internet services clearly enjoy certain economies of scale and scope: significant numbers of users lower production and distribution costs, and awareness and breadth of use offer increasing returns. This suggests that while some small, boutique telecenters may be able to realize economic self-sustainability, most will be hard-pressed to leverage any economies and will suffer from higher costs and less content.

As PCs become more and more like commodities and profit margins go towards zero, economies of scale associated with purchasing PC hardware begin to vanish. However, infrastructure, particularly for the Internet, benefits significantly from economies of scale. For satellite-based connectivity, savings are realized in particular when scale is achieved in the space segment. Here also, however, such scale economies are diminishing as new technologies and business models support smaller deployments.

For terrestrial systems, economies of scale are enjoyed as the number of subscribers increase per radio access tower erected, or copper or fiber cable laid. The corDECT system, a

Wireless Local Loop (WLL) technology manufactured by the Midas Corporation, is an example that demonstrates these scale economies. Economies of scope allow revenues and risks to be spread over a variety of potential sources. One of the strengths of the community computer center model is that it easily allows for such economies of scope.

The costs for power, rent, salaries, and so forth are all shared across a variety of services, such as entertainment and communication. The cost to the operator to deliver each additional service approaches zero, yet it may attract additional users. As service offerings become more diverse and context-appropriate, use becomes more intensive, and as more users within that society access these services, the need for educating new users decreases, while risks of offering service are distributed more widely across the community.

The creation and implementation of innovative business models that are low cost, dynamic, and responsive to local needs in their delivery of ICTs is at the core of achieving economic viability and creating value for the community. As mentioned in the introduction, economic self-sustainability of the Internet in rural areas over the next few years will depend on one key business decision: making facilities shared, rather than focusing on individual use.

For instance, Internet services and facilities are provided at multipurpose community telecenters or telekiosks. These facilities aggregate the demand of an entire rural community, take advantage of economies of scope, and can be situated in existing structures (e.g., temples, schools, government offices, and small markets), thus reducing recurrent costs, while increasing traffic and helping to integrate the facility into the social fabric of the community.

Rural Service Provider (RSP)

Professor Ashok Jhunjhunwala of IIT-Madras to develop local Internet and telephone business models in rural India that are small, entrepreneurial, and leverage the informal sector, while also achieving economies of scale and scope. These businesses will look very much like the Indian rural cable television operators described earlier. In this business format, a local entrepreneur is able to quickly and inexpensively receive a license as a Rural Service Provider (RSP).

Such providers can offer computer applications, Internet services, and basic telephone services through public access centers (which are effectively franchises) and private connections, and use some combination of WLL, fiber, VSAT, or other technologies to connect to networks operated by an ISP and/or other telecommunications companies.

The RSP license would require fair and equitable revenue sharing between the rural provider and a major formal-sector basic service operator such as the incumbent voice provider. The RSP business model allows small and informal-sector enterprises, operating with extremely favourable cost structures and committed to providing high levels of local service, to offer very economical rural ICT services via telecenters.

The combination of the entrepreneur's flat cost structure, service commitment, and understanding of the local market, together with other like entrepreneurs or RSPs who can offer the aforementioned benefits of scope and scale is at the core of this model. It is also significant that the RSP model will be able to help governments and telecommunications companies achieve universal access by offering voice telephony in rural areas at a cost and level of service that is currently unachievable in many communities.

Indeed, many incumbents require or request subsidies to serve these markets, thus squandering scarce resources and opportunities for smaller and local entrepreneurs, and often leading to poor service at a high cost with questionable economic sustainability.

Combining telekiosks with existing organizations can indeed lower recurrent costs while sharing capital costs across more users and services. In the case of a school (exemplified by the World Links example described earlier), an administration may offer the computer lab for community use in the school's off hours, thus ensuring more effective use of infrastructure and resources and generating revenues to help pay recurrent costs.

Alternatively, an operator may sell blocks of time, instruction, or services in her cybercafé to local institutions such as schools, businesses, and hospitals. These institutions have better resources than individual families, and they can thus be used as a sort of anchor tenant, allowing the establishment of a base level of income in the cafe while providing a valuable service to the community. As part of the Schools Program in Tamil Nadu, the government issued a tender to private companies to create computer labs and offer instruction in all twelve hundred public higher secondary schools.

Private operators retained ownership of the equipment (and responsibility for its functioning) and were able to supplement the state fees by using the facilities to generate additional revenue outside of nonschool hours. Telecenters will also improve viability by delivering an extended suite of services relevant to the community, depending on the available information infrastructure and human capital.

In other words, in addition to providing online access to information and communications, they may also offer ICT training, business center services, computer repair, Web design, and back office services such as accounting. The basic premise is that their capacity, both technical and human, should be leveraged fully in order to best use these resources. Capital goods, such as hardware, quickly depreciate, some or all Internet costs are fixed, and employees must be paid regardless of their work level; savvy business owners will, therefore, seek ways to keep their workers and equipment fully employed. Full employment will not only generate additional revenue, but also gradually may help move the business and its capabilities up the value chain. At a community level, the range of services offered creates greater acceptance of ICTs and further embeds them within the social and business culture.

Rural-urban cooperation

Relationships with organizations from outside the community, whether by formal business ties, investment, or grants, can play important roles in financial viability. Private sector supply-side participation is a key component for entrepreneurs' access to capital, equipment, networks, applications, and expertise. Likewise, developing this cooperation improves access to previously hard-to-reach rural markets for these organizations, allowing them to serve new consumers, build networks, and create new economies of scale and scope.

These considerations present potential dilemmas from a development perspec-tive, because there may be a tendency to locate facilities in wealthier areas, advertise in the language and location of certain consumer groups, or create an atmosphere that is unwelcoming to particular members of the society. One important safeguard against business owners taking this approach is a genuine potential for competition, which may make them more inclined to maximize their market share.

Varied regional experiences and limited relevant data do not allow us to suggest a systemic solution. It is important for development organizations and government to remain vigilant in order to stem increased disparities in access to ICT.

Shared access models have been able to operate in many different regulatory environments, but have depended on flexibility to address market needs within the existing framework, regardless of whether the framework appeared welcoming. Telecenters exist where there is a state-owned monopoly provider and where there is complete openness and competition. They offer VoIP when they are able, and chat and e-mail when they are not. The telecommunications policy and regulatory framework as well as the overarching business environment present key opportunities for, and challenges to, rural ICT provision in general, and the telecenter model in particular.

These factors affect everything from investment in infrastructure to availability of capital, and directly and indirectly dictate the range and profitability of services. The number and nature of the participants in the telecommunications industry affect costs, speed, and service quality and have substantial financial and business model implications for providers. Generally speaking, competitive environments and multiple backbone providers will offer lower costs and higher service quality and range, and be more inclined to create and adapt to a dynamic communications environment.

Large telecommunications companies are attracted to large urban areas, and are reluctant to enter smaller and rural markets where they are less profitable and often lose money. Governments have required and cajoled them to serve these areas through a combination of service requirements and subsidies, but have had limited success in creating competitive rural markets. In much of the developing world, rural access remains limited in scope, consistency, and quality.

New entrants typically give priority to the lucrative urban markets, and may meet rural service requirements with infrastructure that is insuffi-cient for effective Internet access. While Peru's fixed line telephony market is officially liberalized, for instance, incumbent Telefónica del Perú offers the only wire-line service outside Lima. Monthly rates for leased lines to tele-centers are US$560 for 64 Kbps and US$780 for 128 Kbps, and many operators complain about bottlenecks, delivery at much lower speeds, and slow response to problems.

Informal surveys suggest that telecenters in Lima, where there are multiple service providers, were more likely to lease faster connections, and pay lower rates. Some operators outside Lima reported that they were reluctant to switch to satellite service, fearing that it would be inadequate for the needs of their business and that, upon returning to the incumbent, the operators outside would be punished. The results are that line costs comprise nearly half of spending for most telecenters in smaller cities, and that the increasing commoditization of Internet access means service problems result in not only lost business, but also lost customers.

Some Indian private sector Basic Services Operators (BSO) are experimenting with variations of the aforementioned RSP model because of government requirements to serve entire Indian states, including rural areas. By effectively subcontracting a smaller company with a flatter cost structure to deliver service in these less appealing markets, the private sector BSOs hope to be able to meet their service coverage targets more efficiently. For their part, RSPs have a direct incentive to offer a context-appropriate range, cost, and quality of service, are able negotiate their coverage obligation, and would not be required by the central government to post a cash guarantee.

Regulatory barriers in rural service

Many regulatory regimes are designed to address for large operators primarily interested in delivering service in urban areas, and certain requirements have negative implications for operators interested in rural areas. The specific regulations governing entry into telecommunications services that have particularly profound cost implications for rural operators include universal service and access requirements (to deliver service to a broad geographic area-i.e., an entire state or country-at a certain level of density), cash deposit requirements (this is particularly harmful for less profitable markets and medium term market development strategies), and wireless spectrum allocation (which may effectively punish rural operators because of the lower user density).

A strong and independent regulator is commonly held to be one of the cornerstones of a competitive and efficient telecommunications market, and while reforms are showing progress, there are still significant deficits related to the size and resources of many monopolies, including their national political and economic significance, and the relative inexperience of many regulatory entities. In this age of telecommunications convergence, the policies for service classification determine which services operators at any level are permitted to deliver, and the technologies that they may use to do so.

The most relevant considerations here are whether or not Internet service provision is considered a value-added service and operators are allowed easier entry (as opposed to the common barriers for basic telephony, for instance), whether VoIP is legal (it is not, in many cases), and if it is legal, whether it is considered a data or voice service.

Requirements for universal access can be key drivers for government and telecommunications providers to reach rural areas, but because rural markets are not as appealing as urban ones, providers tend to neglect them. Setting appropriate and attainable target service levels has proved difficult, and enforcing timetables has been equally so.

Countries are experimenting with new regulatory approaches that blend rural service incentives and requirements, with many nations instituting telecommunications taxes that reserve a portion of earnings for rural service subsidy. In Bolivia's recent market opening, no-fee licenses were offered in exchange for commitments to rural service and education. Chile created a fund for rural service to attract private operators who, upon closer study of the market, actually determined that no subsidy was necessary.

Many smaller ISPs must expect uneven regulatory enforcement, and are frustrated by the unpredictability of their environment. One of the central and most difficult challenges facing smaller ISPs is that of ensuring timely interconnection between national carriers, regional providers, and telecenters, all at fair rates. Both actual interconnection and rate setting are essential for competition, particularly where one carrier is the primary holder of the infrastructure, but have proved difficult even in developed markets where regulatory capacity is greater, and should be accorded significant attention.

While many rural Internet facilities depend on "always-on" connectivity for access to the Internet, some use dial-up connectivity. The negative impact of time-metered calls for Internet access, versus the flat rate used in the U.S. or discounted rates in Chile, Colombia, and elsewhere, cannot be underestimated. Metered rates in many Latin American nations, for instance, effectively double the cost of Internet access.

The drastically reduced costs of VoIP represent a significant financial threat to long distance and international service incumbents, and a tremendous revenue source for telecenter operators and RSPs. Many governments are wary of reducing incumbents' overall revenues, whether by diminishing income from outgoing international long distance or changing the balance of incoming versus outgoing international calls.

Developing nations commonly have as much as four times more incoming traffic, and this generates substantial earnings from call termination fees. VoIP can drive communication costs down rapidly, while providing much needed revenue and foot traffic for telecenters. The metrics of urban areas are commonly used for wireless spectrum allocation procedures and calculations of rates, and are accordingly inhospitable to rural operators.

Rural areas typically have lower population and business densities and higher rates of poverty, and these characteristics likely translate into both lower user density and fewer users per capita. It is important to reconcile these practices in order to take advantage of the opportunities for wider service and more competition in rural areas that wireless technologies present. Spectrum needed for wireless technologies in rural areas may also be allocated for other purposes, and therefore unavailable, even if it is in fact unused in the rural areas that require it most.

Businesses are subject to a series of ongoing interactions with both government and financial institutions. Important broad considerations for new businesses include ease of starting a business registration procedure (registration procedures, time required), ease of running a business (burden of reporting, time spent with government, relevant labour laws), and cost of running a business (import duties, taxes). Regardless of how positive the business climate may be, new businesses and their clients must be able to access funding on fair terms from banks, the government, private equipment or service providers, or from other lenders.

Rural entrepreneurs may face greater hurdles in accessing capital through these sources than those in urban areas, both because of the perceived novelty of their request and because rural entrepreneurs may be unfamiliar with formal financial institutions. Nonprofits, such as India's Dhan Foundation, have developed programs to assist their self-help groups in applying for loans from banks and government programs.

Mechanisms and legal provisions for billing, settling accounts, issuing credit/smart cards, and transferring funds determine the appropriateness, cost, and quality of certain services (e.g., e-commerce, national and international remittances). This business backdrop is a combination of government policy, the legal and regulatory environment, and practices within financial institutions, and therefore depends on diverse stakeholders to ensure its effectiveness.

There is a clear consensus among development professionals that training and capacity-building are key components for telecenter success. Some of the main elements of capacity-building and effective functioning of telecenters can be broken down into the major areas of business skills, ICT skills, employee management, and outreach skills. As with any other business, basic techniques for business management and account tracking, some of which may be ICT-enabled, are essential for running a telecenter.

Small businesses often operate in an informal way, which makes important processes such as tracking spending patterns and sources, income sources, and costing, difficult. These practices negatively impact available information for managers, and therefore the decision-making and planning process, which is particularly important when offering and developing a new suite of services (and paying associated costs).

Poor or incomplete records and substandard management practices adversely affect relationships with existing or potential funders, who expect (and reward) complete and accurate records. Operators require a sound understanding of the potential and uses of ICT, as well as the skills necessary to explain and deliver services to their users; operators effectively act not only as a provider, but also a champion.

To capitalize on their knowledge of the local community and its ICT needs, it is important for operators to understand available ICT tools, identify the resources needed to deliver the level and type of service necessary, and to design the associated business model. Unlike more traditional businesses in which products are more widely understood, employees may be called on to act as guides and facilitators for those unfamiliar with the technology.

Managers must be able to inspire enthusiasm for ICT, as well as teach their employees the skills to instruct users. Secondary school and college students are adept facilitators, and are often willing to either volunteer or work in a telecenter at relatively low wages, in exchange for ICT access. These types of arrangements, however, may generate a new set of challenges to managers. Outreach, marketing, and interaction with the community are key elements to achieving the economic sustainability of a shared resource; if word of available services does not reach wide enough or is met with resistance, success is unlikely.

Outreach efforts will include businesses, individuals, nonprofit and public organizations, as well as civil society groups. Creating awareness, interest, understanding, and acceptance of these new technologies is challenging, particularly in rural areas, and these components have often been closely linked to training. Red Científica Peruana offers an example at the entrepreneur level. The company held training sessions for telecenter operators on a weekly basis at its own telecenters for years, offering free advice and support to anyone who was interested in setting up a telecenter.

Bibliography

Beckner, Weldon; Bruce Barker "Technology in Rural Education", Phi Delta Kappa Education, 1994

Freitas, Deborah L. Inman, "Managing Smallness : Promising Fiscal Practice for Rural School District Administrators, Eric Clearinghouse on Rural Education and Small Schools, 1993.

Howley, Craig B., "The academic effectiveness of small-scale schooling (an update), Charleston", W. Va. : Clearinghouse on Rural Education and Small Schools, Appalachia Educational Laboratory, 1994

Howley, Craig B.; Aimee Howley "The power of babble: technology and rural education", Phi Delta Kappan, v77 n2 p126(6), Oct 1995.

Randall, Ruth E., "Trio of Telecommunications Projects Are Paradigms for Rural Education", T.H.E. Journal: Technological Horizons in Education, (18) 10, 1991.

Thomas G., Tate, "Learning networks: looking to 2010", The Annals of the American Academy of Political and Social Science v529 p71(9), 1993.

VanSciver, James H., "Promoting technology in less wealthy rural districts", School Administrator (52) 28-30, 1995.

VanSciver, James H., "Using a strategic plan to promote technology in less wealthy rural school districts. T.H.E. Journal: Technological Horizons in Education (22) 72-3, 1994.

Webb, Clark D.; Larry K. Shumway; R. Wayne Shute, "Local Schools of Thought : A Search for Purpose in Rural Education", ERIC Clearinghouse on Rural Education and Small Schools, 1996

Index